Land of July

A Real Life Scandal of Sex &

Social Media at a Connecticut High School

Robert M. Marchese

Black Rose Writing | Texas

ISBN: 978-1-68433-076-8
PUBLISHED BY BLACK ROSE WRITING
www.blackrosewriting.com

Printed in the United States of America
Suggested Retail Price (SRP) $18.95

Land of July is printed in Traditional Arabic

This book is strangely yet lovingly dedicated to each and every one of my students – past, present, and future – for whom I have nothing but the most humble and earnest intentions.

"All I can do is write about it."
– Lynyrd Skynyrd

"…and my stomach kind of fell as I felt how hard the world was
going to be to me hereafter."
– John Updike ("A&P")

Land of July

Foreword

It always strikes me when someone marvels over the salacious or unbelievable nature of a story and declares how "You can't make this stuff up." I nevertheless nod my head and politely agree. But I secretly scoff at this notion and think to myself: "*I* could. I could make that up. What's so difficult about that?"

I'm not the handiest of men. I can't build or repair furniture. I don't know the first thing about cars. And after being a homeowner for most of my adult life, I still need to take a minute before distinguishing between the boiler and the hot water heater. Pathetic, I know.

What I can do is use my imagination. It's likely my best and most treasured asset. When I was a little boy I would make up scenarios, and in fact entire *worlds,* with my older sister, Amy, causing her to marvel with amusement – and perhaps a little concern – over the inane hilarity that bounced endlessly around her brother's brain.

As I matured – a word I always use loosely in the first person context – I found myself relying more heavily on imagination. Sure, I played sports and studied martial arts and chalked up a few modest accomplishments here and there, yet I always felt that my creative mind was my best tool. It was inevitable to test myself into learning whether I could actually *create* something – something with emotional resonance and maturity. A pretty heady task for a guy whose biggest and brainiest creative contribution had hitherto been contriving absurd stories to unsuspecting girls in bars.

So I began writing songs and short stories and even jokes. Suffice it to say, much of it was awful. The songs were pale Bob Dylan rip-offs; the stories were callow attempts to be profound; as for the jokes, they simply weren't that funny.

I'm a late bloomer. And how apropos that I even discovered *this* later in life. It therefore took me a while to write anything that was halfway decent. But I kept at it, and found, by the time I reached my mid–twenties, that I was not only getting better, but that I was getting good. Moreover, I had some things to say. My heart had been broken a few times, my parents mounted a nasty year–long divorced, and I went through enough requisite tumult to give me fodder for my writing.

The aim of any writer is, naturally, to expose truth. Such a lofty endeavor. An arrogant one as well. Whoever claims to know any truths of human existence is, in a way, intimating that they are among the chosen ones, that they have been shown the secret, ancient documents inscribed with Godly wisdom, and that this wisdom can be illuminated however they see fit. But the fact remains: You *must* tell the truth. Otherwise, it's just words and images. That's as useful as a compass is to a blind man.

My first major published work, a novel entitled *Nine Lies*, is, ironically, full of the truth. When I'm asked what inspired me to write the book, my response is always the same: what it means to me to be a man, a father, a son, and the confusion that accompanies such enterprises. These are matters I thought of while writing the book, which I dedicated lovingly and tersely to *The Boys*, meaning my son, my father, and my grandfather. And they're matters I still think about. Every day, in fact.

After *Nine Lies* was published in the winter of 2014, I began plotting my next project. I envisioned a novel whose protagonist would be a stand–up comedian, something I knew a little about after humbly trying my hand at the art form. After a four–page outline, I put the idea aside. I wasn't ready to write another novel. Not just yet anyway. Perhaps I can write a play, I thought. Much shorter than a novel. So I reread a book on playwriting and got to it. After a handful of pages, I lost interest. The natural default medium for me has often been songwriting. Because I don't write terribly intricate tunes, I can accomplish a finished product in only a few days. I was therefore more than content to focus on music during the dreadful winter weather. But it wasn't long before my energies were interrupted by a tremendous groundswell that hurled me into quite the nasty abyss.

Jack London once said that "You can't wait for inspiration. You have to go after it with a club." Yet exactly one week into the new year, on January 7th, 2015, just three days before my fortieth birthday, inspiration came at *me* with a club. I wasn't looking for it, and I sure as hell didn't ask for it or even want it. I use the word "inspiration" very loosely. It may as well be supplanted with "tragedy" or "disaster."

Semantics aside, I was given a story. A *real life* story. One that I earned the hard way. One I didn't have to make up with contrivances. And one that would be as personally devastating as it would be shocking. I'm entirely unapologetic in admitting that writing a book about it occurred to me even during the most brutal moments of my travails. It did. In fact, it's that very notion that sustained me when I thought I might go mad, or commit some heinous act of retribution, or get arrested again.

Yes, I would write about it. And in doing so, I would carve out a hideous malignant tumor from my life, a tumor the size of more heartache and loss and humiliation than I ever thought I'd know. A tumor that otherwise might have festered and morphed into something wild and uncontrollable. That's what this book is. It's a tumor. One that I've lived with now for far too long. I've studied it in the most horrible light and in the darkest of hours when the sun and moon became vaporous apparitions.

It's grotesque to me to admit that through all the sorrow the events told in this book have caused, the story they belong to *is* a very entertaining one. What a thought. So sad. This might very well lead some to believe that I have chosen to capitalize on such an ordeal. Some might call me callous or opportunistic. Believe what you will. All I know is that prior to the events told of in this book, someone like me had no business writing a memoir. I'm not a war veteran or a world traveler. I'm not ethnically interesting or the son of an Alzheimer's casualty. I'm a white, middle class father, English teacher, writer. I live in the suburbs. I play music with some of my closest friends. I take care of my body and my brain. I choke on my own breath when I contemplate the love I have for my two children. And my life, up until January 7th, 2015, was mostly peaceful, and utterly private. Up until that point, I was entirely content to simply *make up* my own stories.

A few final words: I realize that this foreword might be regarded as an admission of my propensity to fabricate. It might even be seen as a self-indictment that I am loathe to tell the truth, and that my imagination, an obvious point of pride, is a double edge sword. This is not the case. I won't delude myself into thinking that I can declare, as F. Scott Fitzgerald's narrator did in *The Great Gatsby* that "I am one of the few honest people that I have ever known" and expect to get away with it. Let me posit that I simply have nothing to gain in turning the events told of in this book into some pliable currency for which I might use to procure pity or possibly vindication for any of my actions. I was told throughout my ordeal that *I* was the victim, a thought that always silenced me with unease and disgust. I cannot think of a more abhorrent lot in life than being a victim. Nothing about it appeals to me; from the doleful looks of strangers to the generic "You'll be back on your feet in no time" platitudes, it's as dreadful a lot as I can imagine. Just as I have nothing to gain in compromising the truth, I suppose it can be said that I have nothing to lose as well. So much has already been lost. This perhaps puts me at a sort of emotional stalemate. All I can say is that this story was already acted out. I am merely transcribing it for posterity. This brings me to my final notion: I answer only to my children.

Chapter 1

It was 1:00 p.m. when the bell rang for period 6. A group of students loitered by the far window, sliding their fingers over their phones, speaking in hushed voices. Some stood by their desks and commiserated over an impossible Chemistry test they swore they had just failed. Others sat in their seats, straining to listen to the afternoon announcements that advertised cancelled sports practices and unsafe driving conditions due to the unrelenting January snowfall. It was exactly one week into the new year and predictions were made that we would be looking forward to an unruly winter.

I was thumbing through my copy of Jon Krakauer's *Into the Wild*, searching for a particular passage that would be a precursor to my lesson, when the classroom phone suddenly rang.

"Rob, we need you to come to the main office – right now," the voice said.

Nancy, God love her, had a habit of making everything seem urgent, so I took her unnerved tone in stride. Not only was she the principal's secretary, but Nancy was the eyes, ears, and nose of Daniel Hand High School.

"What about coverage for my class?"

"T.J. wants to meet with you – right now, please."

By the time I hung up the phone, the announcements were over and my students were in their seats.

"I need to leave for a few minutes," I told my class. "I'll be in the main office."

Usually a spirited bunch of 11th graders, they said nothing as I walked out of the room, leaving them in the care of Barb, my paraprofessional. Moving briskly down the hall, I couldn't help but have a flashback to those many long treks to the principal's office when I was a student a couple of decades earlier. Just then a girl walked by and offered a meek smile that made me feel like some benign trespasser. The same thing happened with the next student I passed. And the next. By the time I reached the main floor, I found myself walking towards the unforgettable Mikelle. Mikelle, known by her peers and teachers as that wonderfully idiosyncratic girl, has a tender heart and always speaks her mind. She'll drop five f-bombs in one sentence, half-covering her mouth each time, and then after a few non-sequiturs, giggle and apologize before fist-bumping you on your way.

"Hey, Mr. Marchese," she said, her voice flat and barely audible.

"Hey, Mikelle."

Then, in a seamless gesture that was as sweet as it was uncanny, Mikelle kissed the tips of her fingers and waved them at me.

"T.J. would like you to wait in Cindy's office," Nancy said when I approached her desk in the main office. "He's in a meeting at the moment."

"What's going on?"

"He's asked that you wait in Cindy's office."

"Why?"

"He just needs you to wait."

Her eyes were heavy, her voice soft and maternal. Before doing what I was told, I stepped away from Nancy's desk and peered into the window on T.J.'s office door. He was sitting at his conference table with a male student, the superintendent, and an unidentified man. The student was closest to the door. His expression was solemn and focused.

"Rob, please," Nancy said, her tone gentle and controlled.

Hardly concealing my impatience, I turned and moved in the direction of my vice principal's office. She was not there, so I picked up her phone and called my wife's classroom, thinking she might be able to shed some light on what was going on. It rang several times before Jess, the school's security guard, answered, her voice booming and pleasant. When I asked to speak with Allison, I was told that she was not there. I paced the small room for a minute or two, doing laps around a tiny circular conference table. Then I called back. Still not there. Within a few moments, Cindy appeared:

"What's going on?" I asked.

"I honestly don't know."

"You don't know?"

"I'm sorry."

"This is brutal."

Cindy sighed and shook her head. Always ready with a corny quip or an endearing gesture, she was now all business. I'd always been at ease in her company, but her seriousness was causing me unrest.

"I'm sorry," she said again, leaving me alone after a few moments.

I paced some more before calling my wife's room for the third time. Jess answered again. Looking at my watch, it was 1:15. Time was moving too slowly. Stepping out of Cindy's office, I walked around in circles, gritting my teeth and sighing. After some time, I sat in one of the chairs reserved for students who await their fateful meeting with administration. In an effort to distract myself, I studied the fleet of secretaries who were all either typing away or taking phone calls. They paid me no mind. Just then, a far door opened and Steve, a colleague of mine, walked into the office and sat down. He was still and silent and spoke to no one. My attention was upon him. It took only a moment for me to remember that Steve was not only a well-liked and respected math teacher, but a union rep as well.

Within the next few minutes, I watched through a wide bank of windows as a police car pulled up to the front of the building. Watching the plainclothes officer climb out of his vehicle and enter the main office was like watching an avalanche and having no intention of running for cover. I knew he was entering Daniel Hand High School to become involved in my life. I knew he and I would exchange words and that I would hate everything he had to say. The cop, a stocky, baby-faced man in his mid-thirties, walked past me and into a conference room across the hall from T.J.'s office. By the time I looked at my watch again, it was approaching 1:30. My children. That was my new thought. Something dreadful has happened to my children.

"Steve, what's going on?" I asked when I finally had the nerve to approach him.

The worn look on his face betrayed a controlled kind of disquiet lurking somewhere within him.

"I don't really know all that much," he said.

Poor bastard. He was yanked out of his classroom and given the burdensome vantage point of a front row seat to view the end of a fellow man's life.

"Can you tell me *anything*?"

Pausing a bit, he looked up at me with the kind of sadness you keep on reserve for widows and martyrs.

"It's not about *you* directly," he said.

"Is it my kids? Please tell me it's not about my kids."

Bracing himself a little, he shifted in his seat and told me in his most avuncular voice that it was about Allison. Before I could even respond, let alone process this, Phil, the school's resource officer, appeared from a nearby door and was making his way towards the conference room to join his fellow cops. Tramping through the halls of DHHS Monday through Friday, Phil can be seen beguiling indifferent teenagers to keep out of trouble, and then seconds later debating sports and movies with the dozens of teachers who welcome the respite of his effortless conversation.

"Phil, what can you tell me?"

"I'm not sure, bro," he said, "you gotta just sit back and wait it out."

"What the hell."

"Just sit tight."

I ended up waiting another thirty minutes to the end of the school day. In that time, I called my wife's classroom again and again – she never answered – paced some more, and conjured scenarios that had peaceable resolution to them. Here's one: Allison engaged in a verbal sparring match with an obnoxious student and let it slip that she thought he was a major-league asshole and couldn't stand his presence; the kid then lost his shit and called mom and dad who wasted no time in filing a harassment suit. Or maybe it just came out that she had given answers to some standardized test the year before; certainly this was frowned upon, but once the investigation cleared, it would go down as an indicator of her unerring allegiance to her students' performance. My brain, rooting itself in some makeshift orbit where it played tricks with pity and hope and reason, seemed to allow for this temporary reprieve of unreal daydreams. I knew the matter was of enormous consequence. After all, the cops had been called.

"Rob, come on in," T.J. said, seconds after his meeting ended.

A stoic individual without a trace of self-doubt, T.J. is the kind of man – and boss – who might as well thrive on dealing with chaos since he does so with such mastery. At just under six feet tall, with his impeccable hair combed back and his black pinstripes sleek and pressed, T.J. always struck me as a man with a personal library of a dozen or so motivational books with words in the titles like "Lead," "Power," and "Win."

I entered his office and closed the door. The student and unidentified man were gone. I was alone with T.J. and Tom, Madison's superintendent, a pleasant, gregarious man who most everyone in the district was still trying to figure out. Clean-cut and bright-eyed, he and T.J. look as though they could be brothers.

"We've got a situation," Tom said. "Please sit down."

•   •   •   •   •

My drive home was a maddening seven minutes of unfocused anxiety. I had no idea what to expect once I arrived. A ransacked house with no sign of Allison. A suicide. A study in disbelief over false accusations.

I pulled my car into the driveway adjacent to my wife's silver CRV. Then I sat there for a moment and listened to my heavy breathing. It became the only way I knew I was still alive. When I entered the house, I was met with a deadly quiet. And though there was no sign of Allison, she must have heard my arrival. I thus imagined that the noises I was making were as unsettling to her as the score of a horror film. The opening of the electric garage door. The hum of my car's engine. My footsteps on the hardwood floor.

Dishes from the waffles my children had eaten that morning were on the kitchen counter. I could smell the faintest hint of the maple syrup

I had heated up for them. When I made my way upstairs, I found a distraught and shrunken middle-aged woman sitting on a sofa in the playroom, surrounded by balled up tissues, awaiting a conversation with her husband she never imagined having.

"What did you do?" I said when I found her.

Her expression was drawn and her face was blotchy with tear stains. Next to her was our home phone and a yellow legal pad. On the adjacent sofa was a package of guitar strings and a butterscotch colored Telecaster I hadn't gotten around to restringing. Sticking out from underneath the guitar was a sheet of paper with lyrics to a recent song I had finished and played for Allison the night before. She told me she loved it more than any other I had written. Though this was merely hours ago, it suddenly seemed like some burnt out half-memory made up of some half-assed nostalgia trip.

"It's not that bad," she said.

"What did you do?"

"They're accusing me of having a relationship with a male student."

"*Two* male students."

Naturally, she had no idea the substance of the meeting I had just minutes earlier with our bosses as well as the Madison Police. *Two* boys - possibly more. Serious allegations. Confiscated iPhone. FBI involvement. Multiple investigations underway. These were phrases used to me in the gravest of ways.

"That's what they're saying," she said.

"Forget what they're saying. Is it true?"

Wiping her eyes with a tissue, she was buying some time.

"Is it true?" I asked again.

"It's not as bad as what they're saying."

"What who's saying? What the fuck are you talking about?"

"The boys."

"So there *are* two boys."

"Yes, but they're lying."

Her voice, soft and controlled, must have been working independently from the rest of her.

"They're *lying*? Why would they do that?"

"I don't know."

"You don't know?"

"Things got out of control."

The mere suggestions that lived inside that phrase were as vast as they were sordid. I suddenly felt as though I had to do something with my hands. So I began kneading the tips of my thumbs into my palms as though I was seconds away from frostbite.

"Explain," I said, eyeing my stringless guitar and wishing I could play it.

It's always been too easy to know when my wife is lying. Her eyes are unblinking and her lips vacillate between curling into the faintest smile and the most self-effacing frown. Her words are chosen as carefully as though she's convinced she can use each of them only once. The second the lie has been told, she appears spent and confused.

All the signs were there as she told me a tale about a boy she taught for the past two years – let's call him Gabe – with whom she claimed she at one time had a friendly rapport. Sure, she said, he had followed her on Instagram, which is where they texted a bit, but it was mostly innocuous, sometimes coy, but never lewd. Though I didn't know Gabe, he was a boy she had mentioned to me on multiple occasions, particularly during the current school year when she would reveal that he seemed distant, moody even; this, she would say, was an anomaly since just last year he had liked her so much. The proof, she would often tell me, was how he would make a public showing of his affection by asking her out on dates in front of the class. Practically beaming when she told me these stories, her elation must have given way to contempt over my near silence and utter lack of interest. One time I asked her flat out if she told Gabe this was not appropriate behavior. Her response was nearly defensive:

"It's a running joke. Totally harmless. The rest of the class is in on it. They think it's hilarious."

It suddenly struck me that Gabe was the serious looking student in my principal's office just moments earlier. As it turned out, I was currently teaching Sam, his nearly identical-looking older brother in my Creative Writing course. Bright and gregarious, Sam ingratiated himself to me just a week or so earlier with talk of music and film. The entire family, in fact, possibly one of the most prominent in town, is as high achieving as they are well-respected.

Version #1 of the truth placed much of the onus on Gabe. It was *Gabe* who had initiated contact via Instagram. It was *Gabe* who had pursued her. And it was *Gabe* who had crossed the line, if, she was careful to mention, the line had in fact been crossed at all.

"So you're faulting a fourteen-year-old boy for these interactions."

"He's fifteen."

"Excuse me?"

"He's fifteen."

I stared dumbly at her.

"He turned fifteen this year," she said.

I began kneading my hands again. This time with more friction. Then I launched into the tirade I had launched into nearly every week for the past couple of years.

"You and your phone and your Instagram and your bullshit technology. Now look where it's gotten you."

She knew all too well the point I was making. She knew I loathed her obsession with social media and how she spent nearly all of her free time on her iPhone and iPad and how she was territorial and even rigid when it came to her "followers" and "friends." Facebook. Instagram. Snapchat. Yik Yak. We argued about each one of what I still consider colossal time-wasters. Time-wasters that somehow seem more fitting for teenagers than adults. It's true that at times I could get on my high horse and declare that these outlets were nothing more than pernicious excuses to disengage from real life and real interaction. I suppose I felt justified in doing so since it was these very outlets that had been, for years, sending my wife perilously adrift from her family.

When I asked the nature of her relationship with Gabe, she admitted that she liked him. A lot.

"So you fell in love with a fourteen-year-old boy?"

"No."

"Then what would you call it?"

"I don't know."

"You don't know?"

"I had feelings for him."

"You had *feelings* for him?"

My voice was under control. The genuine curiosity I felt over the matter must have forced civility upon my tongue.

"Yes."

"What kind of feelings?"

She thought about it for a moment; then she said something that most likely freed her of a burden she was carrying for close to a year:

"The only other person I've ever had those feelings for has been you."

"Oh my God."

"But I wouldn't say I *love* him."

"It sounds like you're too embarrassed to call it love. But that's what it seems like to me."

"I don't know *what* to call it."

"*Fucked up*, for starters. For starters, you can call it *fucked up*."

When I asked if she had ever revealed this to anyone, she admitted that several months back she told Christie, one of her younger sisters. Christie's reaction: Put it out of mind and don't act on it.

"How long has this been going on? How long have you been stalking this poor kid?"

She grew pensive.

"How long?"

"Not that long."

"How long?"

After filling her lungs with a gulp of air, she looked me in the eyes and told me it had all begun the year before – in the spring trimester. I let this register, thinking of our life together during the past several months. There wasn't time to collect all the traces of betrayal. So I counted in my mind just exactly how long we were dealing with.

"Ten," I said.

"What?"

"*Ten* months."

"I don't know."

"I do. That's *ten* months. Simple math."

I would no doubt review the previous year with a demented sense of urgency, like I was a p.i. on the cusp of breaking open the case of the century. But that would have to wait. It required too much thinking for the moment. One thought, though, did enter my mind. It was something she had said to me on our way home from the Outer Banks the previous summer, mere months into her affairs. With our children watching *Rio 2* in the backseat, we were somewhere in northern Virginia when talk turned to sex. It was somewhat playful. Erotic even. Then it became strange when the focus shifted to cheating. And with a sober, almost foreign sounding voice, she faced me and said that if I ever decided to cheat on her, it was okay, but to just never let her know about it. This from a woman who had turned jealousy into a mainstay of our marriage. Her insecurities had dominated more conversations and consumed more energy than can be counted. So I was naturally struck by this newfound attitude.

"Ten months," I said again.

She was silent.

"Before you tell me about boy #2, please tell me you didn't do anything with Gabe."

"I *never* touched him. We never did *any*thing."

She said this with such force, such assuredness, that the whites of her eyes beamed and her voice repaired itself temporarily so it would come off as strong and unbroken. She had risen, if only for a moment, and it was as though we were a normal married couple talking about dinner plans for that evening. I believed her. Yet I was hardly hopeful.

The second she uttered boy #2's name – let's call him Zach – my mind was overcome with images of the two of them talking in the halls, joking, laughing, even walking together. Though he was never a student of mine, I knew of him. Zach was older than Gabe, a senior, and, like Gabe, he was a football player. This meant she had spent considerable time with him – with both of them – since she had, for the past few years, trained with the athletes during their summer session. Not to mention, she took an after school job in the school's weight room where she would work out with the students, most of whom were male.

"Zach and I began talking a lot, mostly about his dad," she told me.

I understood what she meant: Zach's father, a local business owner, took his life only months earlier.

"I told him about Amy," she went on.

The previous summer, our friend also committed suicide. It was a loss that left a lot of unanswered questions, as well as Amy's young son without a mother.

I was not at all moved by my wife's commiseration with Zach. It appeared that she was attempting to create a ruse that she was thoughtful and sensitive, but really, the obviousness of it all hung there like a badly broken bone: She preyed on some poor kid's vulnerability for her own gain.

"We just talked."

"And that's it?"

"And we flirted a little."

"Flirted?"

"Yeah."

"So you texted harmless texts with Gabe and had a mild flirtation with Zach, and that prompted the Madison Police to come to our school, confiscate your phone, which they're turning over to the F.B.I., escort you from the building, and initiate an investigation?"

I reminded her of the line she had used earlier in our talk: "Things got out of control." Version #2 of the truth would come soon enough. Its catalyst was my doubt, which I voiced repeatedly. When this proved futile, I said something to unsettle her, something I thought was true, but had no way of knowing for certain:

"I'm going to find out *every*thing. It's all going to come out, so you might as well save us the trouble."

This caused her to squirm in her seat a bit. Yet she maintained her story.

"What else did you do?"

"I told you everything."

"What else did you do?"

"I told you."

"What else did you do?"

"Rob."

"What else did you do?"

The pause that followed created a hideous silence, one that was packed to its absolute limit with grotesque possibility. When it passed, more details were revealed. Zach had paid a visit to her classroom a few weeks back. This happened during her prep period, so she was alone. Once there, they talked a bit. Matters soon escalated and they were in each other's personal space, making out and groping at one another. After she got him off, he cleaned himself up and returned to class.

Allowing her words to settle in my brain, I said nothing for a while. She began to sob. And apologize. This went on for a bit before I seized the opportunity:

"What else did you do?"

"That's it. I swear."

"What else did you do?"

"Rob, I swear."

"What else did you do?"

The conflict she must have had was her conviction over two things: 1) That the full, unadulterated truth would for sure obliterate our marriage, and 2) That my tenacity was as bullheaded as anything she had ever known. She had to have recognized that the dam was broken and the waters were more than just seeping in: They had already carved out a smooth trajectory and were gaining more traction by the second.

What can be said of those brutal moments when you discover that your life will never again be the same from what it has been? They are electrical currents that cause tremors and blackouts to your entire central nervous system. They are flash floods that wash over you, eroding all that has been blessed and safe and familiar. It's a sudden death in the family. It's losing your job or your home or your health. It's finding out that your wife performed oral sex on a minor in her locked classroom, which was just down the hall from your own.

The phone rang shortly after she told me this, so I barely had a chance to respond. On the other line was the union lawyer she had called when she returned home that afternoon. Composed and articulate, she told the attorney that her iPhone had been confiscated by the Madison Police and that she was under investigation for alleged relationships with two male students. There were breaks in the conversation as she took notes on the legal pad. With nothing to do with myself, I set my guitar aside and picked up my song to reread:

"Shelter"

Daylight's coming...coming down, down, down
Like a waterfall running...through this town
You can't stand straight, been trippin' on your heels
You think you sealed your fate by breaking all your deals
You need shelter
You need shelter
You need shelter
You need shelter from the stars, shelter from the sun
You're hiding out, and on the run, you need shelter...from everyone

August moonrise...it shines, shines, shines
Like the love in your eyes...that was mine
You can't sit still, been moving coast to coast
You think you found the will to understand your ghost
You need shelter
You need shelter
You need shelter
You need shelter from the stars, shelter from the sun
You're hiding out, and on the run, you need shelter... from everyone

By the time I finished reading, it dawned on me that this would be the last song I'd ever share with my wife. It was a tradition that had established itself early in our relationship, and one that had been particularly intimate without ever being physical. When it appeared that she would be on the phone for some time, I set the sheet of paper down and cleared my throat loud enough to get her attention.

"Put the call on hold for a second," I said.

She did so without pause. Then she stared up at me with a doleful longing as though she was certain I was about to say something sweet.

"You must be the stupidest person on the planet. Do you know that? You are so fucking stupid for what you've done."

She looked mystified, as though I was an illusionist on the brink of revealing my craft.

"Good luck with your lawyer. You better hope he's good."

With that, I left the room and went downstairs and outside into the garage. Then I got into my car and drove to my children's daycare. In the parking lot, I called my father.

"I need to come over tonight."

"Everything all right?"

"No."

"What's the matter?"

"I'll tell you when I get there. I'm coming with the kids – it'll be just the three of us."

"Will you want dinner?"

"I don't care."

"Well, will you eat?"

"I don't know. I don't care. See you in an hour."

This phone call was an aberration. Never one to impose my burdens on my family, I had, over the years, done well with the business of being an adult. I therefore imagine that my father hung up the phone with the heaviest of hearts. And that he and my stepmother sat on their couch in front of the TV, surmising what it could have all been about. No doubt they ran through all the possibilities. My children. My marriage. My job. My sanity. My future. They would have to be clairvoyants to have guessed that it was exactly all of these.

During the drive, I realized I had no practice when it came to delivering bad news to my family. Mildly unpleasant news, sure. As in "I'm moving to Chicago" or "Looks like I'll be in Canada this Christmas." But nothing like what I was about to reveal. I had a decent track record for getting the job, getting the girl, winning the trophy.

This was going to be mind numbing.

When I arrived at their place, my kids were set up in front of the TV while I brought my father and Helene, my stepmother, into the next room to explain to them what had happened. My father is a man with zero tolerance for innuendo or euphemism, so I came right out with it. I told them about the meeting I had hours before with my principal and superintendent and the Madison Police. I told them about the sick allegations against their daughter-in-law and the conversation she and I had prior to my arriving at their house. My father said nothing. Studying my face, he inhaled deeply a few times and closed his eyes every so often the way he does when disappointment overwhelms him.

"You're staying here tonight," Helene said.

A thoughtful offer, but I refused. I would not be ejected from my home because of my wife's grotesque behavior.

"Robbie, this is not about ego," she said. "It's about the safety of your children. She's not right in the brain – to do what you're saying she did."

In her more delicate moments, my stepmother calls me "Robbie," an affectionate gesture that nevertheless makes me feel twelve-years-old all over again. I held my ground:

"I appreciate the offer, but the kids have school tomorrow – and so do I."

They both looked at me like I had plucked out my eyes in front of them.

"You're going to *work* tomorrow?" Helene asked.

My father stood up and began pacing around the room.

"What choice do I have?" I said. "Go to work and be humiliated or stay home with her and have another miserable heart to heart?"

"What did she have to say for herself?" my father asked.

"Does it matter?" Helene said. "What could she possibly say to make any sense of this? She's not right in the brain."

"What about the kids?" asked my father.

Throwing my arms up in the air, I shook my head and tried to formulate a sentence. Nothing came out. Though his questions might have been impossible to answer, or even contemplate, I knew where he was coming from. He was recognizing that the life I had cultivated with this woman for the last twelve years was already dead and buried, and he was incredulous that, like me, and like the rest of my family for that matter, he had missed the funeral.

Dear Old Life,

To state the obvious: You have been assassinated. This is what I tell people. As if they didn't know. All I understand about assassinations is that they appear to be random, but are often plotted by a meticulous hand. This is the case with how it happened to you. You never saw it coming. I can attest to this. You existed one moment, reveling in your existence, thriving in countless ways, and then you were the stuff of headlines. You were in your prime. Mostly. If we're being truthful, there was a void here and there. But you made up for it with the kids and the music and the writing and the teaching.

The plotting part of your murder is tricky to fully comprehend. We know there was premeditation involved, but not necessarily intent to kill. The intent was duplicity. And had the crimes not been found out, perhaps you might have endured, albeit in a state of absolute oblivion. This is no way to be. But as the saying goes, ignorance is bliss.

I will remember you always and speak fondly of you when you come up in conversation. It's likely that as time passes I will philosophize and ruminate less and less over what happened and how it all went down. It will be important for me to move on. It's no feat to be maudlin over what's been lost. I will need to fight the urge. So I will mourn you with dignity, pay you my respects, and embrace my new life. I know you won't begrudge me this.

Some brief final words need to be put in for the assassin. Quite the sleight of hand she pulled off. Talk about sleeping with the enemy. When I look back, I see now that I spent entirely too much time warning her, and not enough time warning you. Probably because I didn't recognize just how beguiling she was. Not to mention disturbed. But that's always the way with an assassin: They live next door to you. They smile as they take your order. They sell you life insurance. They bear you children and swear to you their loyalty and affection.

Though you can never be replaced, you will be succeeded. I don't state this matter-of-factly or with a light heart. It's just the way it is. God bless.

R.I.P.,

Rob

Chapter 2

So much was made of my return to work the following day. I understand why, I suppose: Most people might have imagined me either taking time off to sort through the wreckage, or maybe they figured it was the end of me, that I was done for, bested by the embarrassment, fated to squander my remaining years in hiding, or worse, begging my wife to please tell me why she had done the unthinkable by destroying our family. I saw my return as nothing more than perfunctory. There was no bravado, no spite, no pride even, in my showing up to work on January 8th. It was visceral, the same way a defeated boxer climbs out of the ring and moves past the crowd, bleeding and barely able to walk upright towards his dressing room. It's nothing more than moving from point A to point B. Both points are sure to be reminders of the kind of disappointment that sucks away your breath and makes your head so light that you swear you'll never have another thought as long as you live. But you can tell yourself that at the very least, movement was accomplished.

I carried with me zero affectation that day. I'm sure there was some primitive hint of stoicism in my behavior, but I was not at all conscious of how I appeared. I was simply trying to not fall over. The first person I saw was the building's friendly Beatles-obsessed custodian who was outside laying salt on the sidewalks. He greeted me the way he always had before. I initialed the faculty sign-in sheet – I was the first teacher in the building that morning – retrieved my mail, and headed upstairs to the third floor. It was early, around 6:15, and the building would be teeming with bodies within the next half hour. As I walked through the empty hallways, the light and the heat struck me in entirely new ways. I felt as though I was walking through some bright wind tunnel and out onto an open runway where I would soon be featured as some pathetic spectacle.

My first order of business was to clean out Allison's classroom. With my master key, I unlocked the door to room 347, the scene of some of her most prominent crimes, and got down to it. I worked furiously at collecting all traces of her. Framed photographs of her and I. Coffee mugs with the word "Teacher" on some of them. Hand lotion and posters and books and knick knacks. Pictures and collages made by Robbie and Riley. Like some fugitive drug lord, I stuffed everything into a few plastic bags, took one last look around, and closed and locked the door.

When I arrived in my own room, I flipped on the lights and hid Allison's things in my closet. Then I turned on some music and began straightening up from having left so early the day before. Every so often, I would walk past my door and look out its window into the hallway, which was slowly filling up with students. Some were sitting on the floor, dozing, listening to music, doing homework; others were standing in clusters, laughing or flirting or eating their breakfast. I imagined that to passersby the light that illuminated from my room must have appeared strange, like seeing sudden signs of life from a house you're expecting to be abandoned. They might have thought that weeds would have sprouted up overnight and that weathered boards would have crisscrossed the doorway, declaring that this was now deserted property.

Even though the tragedy was brand new, I felt like I had instantly morphed into the Boo Radley of the building. Nevertheless, I opened my door, stepped out into the hallway, and walked around with no destination in mind. I was met with smiling faces from everyone in my path; and though I'm sure the smiles were laced with pity and even terror over the thought that I might snap at any moment and storm the building, screaming about my hurt before hurling myself down a flight of stairs, they still gave me what I needed at that moment. Like all consolation, it was makeshift and transitory, but I ate up every last bit of it. By the time the bell rang for my first period class, I was ready to teach – or do something that resembled teaching.

"Good morning," I said to my 11th grade Honors American Literature class.

"Good morning," they said in near perfect unison.

This had become, over the last four months, one of my favorite classes. They were smart, mature kids with great work ethics and senses of humor. We often acknowledged together how unreasonable it was to think deep thoughts and say profound things at 7:30 in the morning, but what choice did we have? On this day, they had an alacrity I knew was rooted in curiosity. Standing there in the front of the room, I allowed silence to take hold for a few moments. I didn't have a planned speech, so I said what came naturally:

"This is strange and things kind of suck right now, but we're all here so I think we just need to attempt to do what we've been doing all year. Is that okay?"

That's all it took for them to nod in agreement and take out their short stories we had been reading. And though I was going through the motions for sure, I managed to remain on my feet for the entire period – and for each one that followed. Nothing spectacular happened that day in the way of teaching or learning. But it was enough for me that my kids showed up and looked me in the eyes and gave it their all to make me forget about what was waiting for me back home.

Many of my students made a point to seek me out during the day and thank me for coming to school. Colleagues checked on me and asked if I needed anything. Some sent me texts telling me they were proud I showed up to work and that it spoke volumes. I texted back "Thanks," which was easier than "It's better than the alternative: sit home and risk a murder/suicide." The principal and his two VPs all dropped by at once to lend their support. It all got to a point where I began to feel sorry for these people who clearly had no idea how they should deal with me. It would be easier, I thought, if I disappeared – maybe steal Robbie and Riley and buy one of those motorhomes and point the thing west and just drive.

As far as what would become of Allison, I could pretty much see her fate fully played out in my mind. It would go down more or less the same with or without me. Terrifying thought. I was superfluous to say the least – a bystander who could writhe and plead and pull out clumps of hair, but it would amount to nothing. The building would still collapse to the ground. The ship would still be split to splinters. The bullet would still lodge in that most crucial space, causing the blood loss to be massive and life altering. She of course saw none of this. Or maybe she did, but decided to downplay the situation with hopeful thinking about best case scenarios and a forgiving community. It's possible, I suppose, that when insurmountable loss looms like it must have for her, the brain gets wily and weird and folds over on itself like an animal seeking protection at any cost. The truth is that when she talked about her fate, she sounded as callow as a child riffing on the notion of becoming a space traveler.

Take that first night, January 7th, when I returned from my father's house. She welcomed me and the kids back like we had gone out for pizza. Not to mention the house was spotless. The granite countertops were gleaming. The appliances had all been wiped down. A load of laundry was freshly folded in a basket at the top of the stairs. I pictured her running around the house, bouncing from room to room, dusting pictures, fluffing pillows, considering whether a clean house might ease the enormous burdens she had just caused.

I didn't speak to her as we put our kids to bed. The truth is that I couldn't even look at her. I found myself sneaking back into my children's bedrooms to lie with them some more. It was as much to get away from my wife as it was to embrace them in what I knew would be an entirely new way. There would be a new moon for the three of us. A new sun. A new sky. We had to fucking relearn the stars all over again.

When I went into my bedroom to change, I found Allison in there, pacing around in small circles. She looked like some bleary eyed traitor who had just been publicly denounced by her motherland.

"Can I talk to you?" she said.

Making someone suffer with rejection can be a game if the argument is slight and the stakes are low. There's time and space for some attitude; things will likely be repaired and restored by the morning at the latest, so why not venture for a little solitude by playing the "fuck you" card. The enormity of our situation precluded any such luxury. I was livid and disgusted, but I was also genuinely curious as to how such things could have happened. This is what prompted me to talk to her that first night. And nearly every night for those three weeks we lived together before I moved out. Not that the conversations were civil on my end – or full of anything resembling compassion. They were not. I spoke to her like I was one of those prime time TV judges and she was some hapless defendant with zero common sense and arrogance to spare.

"What could you possibly have to say?" I said. "That you're sorry?"

"I am. You have to know that."

"You disgrace yourself and destroy our family and all you've got is some bullshit apology?"

"These charges could be dropped," she said. "And life could move forward for us. I know it's hard to see that right now, but it's true. And if that's the case, then the district would pay for all the legal expenses. I spoke with the union lawyer tonight and she told me that. I thought that was good news."

Good news. Two words that had been incinerated from our lives. She was of course blinded by a pitiful need for optimism in the midst of such devastation. Even if that meant sacrificing sound judgment.

"You're fucked. And this family is fucked. And our future is fucked. And it's all because of your vile and vain stupidity."

I ended the conversation by declaring that I would continue to sleep in our bedroom while she made her own arrangements somewhere else in the house. With doe-eyed resignation, she picked up one of the pillows leaning against the headboard and walked out of the room.

"Can I just say one more thing?" she asked, standing in the doorway.

I took a deep breath, sat on the edge of the bed, and waited for what was to follow.

"I will do anything to make this right. Please know that. I'll go to therapy and take meds and do anything you ask of me. Just please please please don't leave me."

With this, she began to cry. Not hysterically. But with loud gasps and real tears that fell down her face and into the corners of her mouth. I sat there and watched this for a bit. Then I stood up and moved slowly towards her. I stopped a few feet away and we stared at one another for a moment. Then I turned my gaze downwards before closing and locking the bedroom door.

•   •   •   •   •

The next three weeks were full of aimless days that seemed to orbit around in quiet confusion, asking nothing of me, and offering as much. I felt indifferent about everything, like a tightrope walker without a net or audience or fear of falling. It was fitting that it was winter. Convenient, too. The constant darkness offered me camouflage when I needed to be invisible. The cold reminded me that I was still breathing.

During my second day back at work, Friday, January 9th, my mother called and asked to meet me at 3:00 at Cohen's, a bagel place not even a mile from my house. We had spoken a bit since the incident broke, but it was time to meet in person. We met at a few minutes before 3:00 and saw that it was nearing closing time. Devon, the girl behind the counter, was a former student of mine. She had graduated DHHS the year before and was home from college on semester break. She let us in and told us to take our time while she cleaned. At a rear corner table, my mother and I sat and sipped water and eased into a hushed conversation as though we were fleshing out a heist.

"How're the kids?"

"They're fine."

"I miss them."

"I'll bring them by soon."

Her eyes emanated a rare kind of light in my direction. It was filled with worry and sadness. This was a look I hadn't seen since her own marriage fell apart decades earlier. In the time since then, there had been only occasional disharmony in our world. No more than any other family. For the most part, though, life had been pretty good. Marriages and births and promotions. We were far from a beleaguered bunch. Now seemed like as good a time as any to break out such a look.

"How are you holding up?" she asked.

"I think I'm in shock."

She nodded.

"Aren't you?" I asked.

"Absolutely. This is unreal. A nightmare."

"Well, brace yourself because it's for real."

"What exactly does she have to say for herself?"

"Does it really matter? What could she possibly say to even begin to explain what she's done. It's a dead-end no matter what she comes up with."

"I understand that, but I need to know *how*, or *if*, she tries to rationalize what she's done. For starters, how did she think she was going to get away with this?"

All good questions. And ones I had already asked Allison. Her answers might as well have been in Farsi; they would have made as much sense to me. One minute she was confused over the suicide of our friend Amy that occurred the summer before; the next she was battling PTSD from childhood woes caused by oftentimes clueless and ignorant parents. To cap these off was off course *my* pivotal role: I didn't kiss her enough; I was too strong a personality; I played out in my band too much, leaving her alone at night to wallow in her delusions that she was some under-appreciated and neglected sex symbol.

"I suppose I've spared you all these years the state of my marriage."

"What's been going on?"

Time was of the essence, so I was selective in what I shared. I stuck to the lighter fare. My wife's massive insecurities and neuroses. Her narcissism and petulance. How she had zero capacity to communicate effectively or cope during times of conflict. My mother knew nothing of her daughter-in-law's anger and self-absorption and immense vanity and materialistic tendencies. She didn't know about the time I was berated for buying our three-year-old daughter pajamas at Walmart. Or how after Hurricane Sandy, I went to the dollar store to buy shampoo and toothpaste for the victims and my wife mocked me and threw a fit over the generic brands I purchased. My mother was ignorant about my wife's chronic skin picking; apparently she had never seen the bloody scabs that lined her hairline and cheekbones, and the scarring that would always ensue after a particularly nasty bout. I told her how it came to pass that I forbade my wife from doing homework with our seven-year-old son; that her condescension and impatience had made him cry too many times to count. I talked about her refusals to re-enter therapy and her panic attacks and OCD and extramarital activities in Canada and her all-consuming obsession with social media.

My mother's silence told me that I might have overwhelmed her. The truth is that I never felt the need to share such intimacies with her. Not for lack of closeness. I trusted her completely and felt comfortable confiding in her. But I had an ally in my father, who naturally seemed a more appropriate sounding board. There's something about two men, especially a father and son, commiserating over their women, comparing notes, and ultimately throwing their arms up in surrender over the timeless divide between the sexes. Throughout the years, he and I would talk on the phone a few times a month. In the beginning, the conversations were full of mostly playful banter, the kind of eye-rolling complaints and innocuous quips that didn't suck the energy out of the listener. But around the time my children were born – six or so years into the marriage – the talks with my father became starker, longer even, and full of heady realizations about my future.

"Sounds like she's been performing all these years," my mother said. "Really playing a character. Putting her best foot forward. You don't go from one extreme to the other overnight. She's been building up to this moment for some time now."

What a sickening thought this was. I ran my fingers through my hair, massaging it into clumps. My mother spoke while I did this:

"We found a lawyer. He's good. Very reputable. I made an appointment with him. I know this is surreal. I know you're confused. But it can't hurt to talk to someone. Even though it's early. I think we should go and hear what he has to say about how things could play out. You have to protect yourself and the kids."

I didn't protest.

"Your sister and I are going to go with you."

As emasculating as this was, I didn't have the confidence to argue.

"I have some food for you and the kids," my mother said when we reached the parking lot.

From the backseat of her car, she produced trays of casseroles and pasta dishes.

"Enjoy," she said. "They've all got plenty of gluten in them."

We both laughed a little, taking perverse pleasure in Allison's allergy.

"Please try to take comfort right now in anything you can," she said. "Robbie and Riley. This food. Anything."

I picked up my kids shortly after that and brought them home. Allison was waiting for us in the kitchen. She welcomed us with a shaky, uncertain voice. I didn't respond.

"Let me help you," she said, taking the trays of food from my hands and studying them for a minute before setting them on the counter.

I sent the kids to play in their rooms. Then I hung my coat in the foyer closet before returning to the kitchen to pack my lunch for the next day. Allison was still studying the trays of food.

"You saw your mom, huh?" she said.

I filled up my water bottle and put it in the refrigerator. Then I made myself a sandwich and wrapped it in aluminum foil. All the while, I ignored her, focusing instead on the sounds of Robbie and Riley playing upstairs.

"I can only imagine the talk the two of you had," she said.

Allison not only had to know every detail of every conversation that took place in her absence, but had a nearly debilitating obsession over what others thought of her. The meeting I had with my mother must have been too much for her to handle. Yet her pride precluded her from asking for specifics. And I volunteered nothing. The doubt she must have been feeling was a result of the only power I possessed: silence.

"That was nice of her to cook for you," she said.

I finished packing my lunch and took a moment to stare coldly at my wife. The sound of the kids moving around some light furniture made its way downstairs. This meant Riley had coerced Robbie into playing what had recently become her favorite game: family.

"Can I ask you something?" she asked.

I waited, anticipating a question I had no plans to answer: "Does your mother hate me?" "Does she think we can work it out?" "Is she encouraging divorce?"

But if any of those matters *were* on her troubled mind, she managed to keep them at bay while she focused on something else entirely:

"Do you know if these are gluten free?" she asked, pointing to the trays of food behind her. "I'm just wondering if we can *all* eat them."

Silence was no longer an option. There were so many ways to respond to what she had said that I was nearly overwhelmed. But I picked one that I thought had the brevity and simplicity the occasion called for:

"You're delusional."

Then I turned from her and followed the sounds of Robbie and Riley.

•   •   •   •   •

Our living arrangement now seems the stuff of dark Hollywood fare. Mealtimes. Bedtimes. Caring for our children. Every routine that had once required collaboration became an impasse, a crucible, a thing of dread. Our kids knew something was amiss. Especially my seven-year-old son.

"It's okay, Daddy," he'd say when I'd interrupt his playing by cupping his little head in my hands and pulling it into my face to kiss him or feel his sweet breath. "Everything's going to be okay."

I wasn't helping the situation by morphing into a catatonic and spending most of my free time in front of the TV on the floor in my bedroom. When I wasn't lounging or sleeping or crying, I was watching documentaries. Mostly on the U.S. and its early years. *The Men Who Built America*, an in-depth look at industrialists like Andrew Carnegie and Cornelius Vanderbilt, and *America: The Story of Us,* a sweeping twelve-part series; these both took days upon days to get through. When I now consider my choices, I'm left with the notion that on a subconscious level I needed to vicariously partake in something that indicated *progress* of any kind. If my real life was mired in something, anything, it was the opposite of progress.

Matters became more bleak for me when Janice, my mother-in-law, dragged her suitcases through our front door. This was a mere few days after the incident broke. My wife announced that her mother would be staying to lend support and had no departure date in mind. In the best of times, I had trouble being under the same roof with Janice for more than a couple of hours. Conversation was nearly impossible unless I could fake it and discuss weather, *Jane Eyre*, or who in her small Canadian mill town had recently gotten "the cancer." The matter went beyond my aversion for small talk. It's true that I loathe it and have no talent for it. But with Janice, there's something more. It's always been this way, ever since I first met her. There's a nervous energy and a constant air of dissatisfaction about her. She doesn't so much breathe as she does sigh; it's as though she's constantly on the verge of either receiving or delivering terrible news.

For the first few days, I managed to avoid her almost completely. She merely flitted about from room to room, cleaning, whistling, and chirping to herself about how she planned on spending the next five minutes of her time. Though cooking was hardly her strong suit, she prepared meals every evening.

"My mother fixed you a plate," Allison would tell me, tracking me down on my spot on the floor in front of the TV.

I had usurped the master bedroom each night while my wife was sleeping on the sofa in the adjacent playroom. Meanwhile, Janice made camp in one of the family-rooms downstairs.

"I don't want it," I said night after night.

"You're not eating," she would say. "I'm getting worried about you."

My silence would eventually send her away. And though I never once ate with my wife and mother-in-law during this time, a plate was always made up for me and left on the table, sealed tight with clear plastic wrap. Often, it would still be there in the morning when I woke.

Allison, now on paid leave from DHHS, stayed home every day with her mother. After they woke and dressed my children and brought them to school, they grocery shopped, watched *Downton Abbey*, and visited Dr. W., Allison's therapist, who she had begun seeing several times per week. I would return home after work to discover that people were starting to come by the house.

One such individual was Dr. H., a local Madison resident who had some serious legal troubles of his own a few years back when he was discovered to have been writing an exorbitant amount of prescriptions to his patients. He was convicted, lost his license to practice medicine, and received five years probation, just narrowly avoiding jail time. Allison took great relief in his visit.

"He said that the people in this town like me and that they'll forgive me," she said. "He pointed out the obvious – that people make mistakes, but can move on. And so can we. We can move on from this."

The dichotomy of forgivable and unforgivable offenses seemed not as evident to her as it was to me. DUI: forgivable. Modest embezzlement: forgivable. Creative prescription writing: forgivable. Preying on teenage boys for close to a year, sending them dirty texts and selfies, and putting their genitals in your mouth on school grounds: not forgivable.

The hope she gleaned from this man was astonishing. Her transformation was enough to cause me to rethink whether we *could* survive this and come out with some rectitude and even a higher understanding of our marriage. Then I would instantly sober up and remember what she had done. Our fate then became as clear to me as though I was viewing it from a short range rifle scope. I wanted to track down this Dr. H.

"What in God's name is wrong with you?" I would have said. "You ignorant, foolish fuck. Your pep-talks sound as useless as your medical license turned out to be. Mind your own business and don't attempt to be a prophet or deal in optimism just because you happen to recognize a fellow narcissist."

Another visitor turned out to be the sister of a colleague of ours; she had always taken a liking to my wife, yet had spent probably a grand total of two to three hours in her presence. She brought with her a dozen yellow roses that stood, crisp and tall, in a vase on the island in our kitchen. A card accompanied the bouquet. It read "Thinking of you and wishing you the very best in these difficult times." No mention of the husband and two innocent children. Preying on young boys and swallowing their bodily fluids gets you a lovely bouquet from this misguided ignoramus. I couldn't help but wonder what full-on intercourse would have garnered: a spa getaway?

Those moments, I now realize, were equally important for both me and Allison. For me, they illuminated a facet of our ordeal I never even considered to be a possibility – that despite what she had done, no matter how grotesque, she had supporters. This became possibly one of the more puzzling pieces of the story. As for Allison, such moments emboldened her. The recognition was thus born that her life would go on and she would flourish, albeit in a far different way than what had once been the norm.

Time moved slowly during those last three weeks my family lived together under the same roof. Much of it was akin to a black comedy. Yet I forced myself into stability and began spending more time with my children. Just the three of us. I still refused to eat meals with my wife or mother-in-law. So we began working in shifts. On Monday, my kids and I would sit at the kitchen table together and eat dinners my mother had made while Allison and Janice watched TV or went shopping. Then on Tuesday, I would hole up in my bedroom while the four of them dined on whatever my mother-in-law had concocted that afternoon.

Time with my children was little more than obligatory. I must have appeared like some melancholy alcoholic in detox, mourning his last beloved drink. All that was missing was the bathrobe and five o'clock shadow. My affection towards them during this time had an almost violent desperation to it, so often erupting into tears I would dismiss as "Tears of joy because Daddy just loves you both so much."

•   •   •   •   •

Without so much as discussing it with Allison, I drove to the Madison Jeep dealer after work one day to trade in the 2015 Wrangler I had purchased a few months earlier. Hardly a car enthusiast, the vehicle, a silver two-door soft top, was nevertheless something I was proud of. It was a token of a recent promotion I had earned at work. The owner of the dealer was the father of a current student of mine and he understood my situation.

"I think I'm going to need a four door," I said.

"Of course."

"Something a bit more practical for young children."

I kept thinking how my kids were excited for May to roll around so we could take advantage of driving a Jeep. Yet this would have to wait for another day.

"And with a lower monthly payment," I added.

"We'll take care of you."

They had a metallic blue Patriot that looked like it would do. I told him I would take it.

"Do you want to test drive it?"

I declined. We filled out some paperwork, made a few photocopies, and he told me the vehicle would be ready the following day.

"Too bad you never got a chance to take the top off the Wrangler."

Offering a meek smile, I merely shook my head, declining to enter into a conversation about the looming prospects of single fatherhood.

•   •   •   •   •

My band had a few shows around this time. We honored all of them. We even kept to our weekly rehearsals in my basement. What had once been a labor of love for me turned into an excuse to get away from my wife for a few hours. The other members of Left on Scarlet Street accepted my sullenness without any misgivings. On the contrary, they embraced me like brothers. Two of them, Dave and Pierre, members of the DHHS faculty, had particularly salient vantage points to my ordeal. And John, our beloved drummer, works in the mental health field, so he understands the depths of the human psyche. I was in good company. Yet they all refrained from being overbearing. And though it was hardly lost on anyone during one particular practice that we were rehearsing a new song of mine I had written for Allison, no one mentioned it. They played their parts and made suggestions on harmonies and fleshed out the tune as though it was just another in our repertoire. The song, "Back to Beautiful," became one we ended up performing on a regular basis.

"Back to Beautiful"

I'm tryin' to come clean / for some time / about my dirty mind
Sun's coming up / like a poisonous pill / been making me go blind
I'm tryin' to wake up / in a river of sin / I'm tryin' to stay in bed
And all my dreams / they're bulletproof, baby / but they're leaving holes in my head

So settle down now/ settle down / settle down now / settle down

And get back, babe...to beautiful...get back to earth and sky
Get back, babe...to beautiful...where all you do is mystify me
Where all you do is mystify me...where all you do is mystify me

This room of ours / is far from Eden / it's far from everywhere
The light is strong / and our time is long / and there's music in the air
Don't pick me up / let me be / leave me in this place
I don't mind at all / if I happen to fall / as long as it's from grace

So settle down now/ settle down / settle down now / settle down

And get back, babe...to beautiful...get back to earth and sky
Get back, babe...to beautiful...where all you do is mystify me
Where all you do is mystify me...where all you do is mystify me

I wanna get high / while you sleep by my side / I wanna float in this flood
I'm going downstream / to get lost in between / your body and your blood
We'll never wake up / we'll never come down / we'll disappear with the dawn

Sun's sinking low / and both of us know / we'll both be forever gone

So settle down now/ settle down / settle down now / settle down

And get back, babe...to beautiful...get back to earth and sky
Get back, babe...to beautiful...where all you do is mystify me
Where all you do is mystify me...where all you do is mystify me

Because of Allison's crimes – at this point, they were "alleged" crimes – DCF would be making a visit to our house. They needed to lay their eyes on our children and make certain they were safe. So one evening, an attractive young woman named Alexandra showed up at our doorstep with a clipboard and a tenuous smile. Prior to her arrival, Allison and Janice cleaned the house, lit scented candles, and changed their clothing. I shook my head, noting the usual dabs of pretense with which they colored things.

Alexandra came inside and met with Allison and I in the upstairs home office. We spoke for a bit while Janice took the kids to play in their rooms down the hall. She asked about our home environment and how we cared for the children and about their schooling and friends and extracurricular activities. I did most of the talking, answering her in a steady, pleasant voice. She took a few notes, but mostly looked at each of us, back and forth, possibly wondering whether she might catch glimpses of the darkness that had enveloped our family.

"Would you mind if I spoke with the kids?" she asked.

"Not at all," I said, not bothering to look at my wife, who then expressed concerns over the prospect.

"It's fine," I said, "this is why you came here tonight. And we intend to cooperate."

Allison thought on this for a minute before retrieving the children from their rooms.

"How are *you* doing, Mr. Marchese?" Alexandra asked once we were alone together.

"I've been better," I said, clutching my iPhone. "But I'm keeping it together."

"I'm sorry for what's happened to your family."

"Thank you."

We stood there for some time waiting for my kids to enter. The moment was filled with a strange energy. But not the kind you flee from. If we were in a movie and not real life, I would have taken a few steps towards her while looking her square in the face. I would have said something like "Is my family the most fucked up one you've seen this week?" And she would have said something like "No, I've seen others more…" before stopping herself. I would have finished her sentence for her: "*Fucked up.*" She would have nodded. I would have mentioned that she must be curious over how things came to be this way for me. She would have said that she was just doing her job by being here this evening. I would have said that I bet it's difficult to always keep things on a professional plane, that she must get emotionally involved at times. Then I would have moved closer to her. All the while we'd be looking at one another. No one would speak for a moment. The scene would end with the tension being broken by my children bounding into the room. Turns out, this became the very thing that obliterated my fantasy.

We introduced Alexandra to Robbie and Riley, telling them she was a friend and just wanted to ask them some questions.

"I love your pajamas," Alexandra said to my daughter. "They're very pretty."

This exchange was what I needed as subterfuge to access the audio recorder on my cell phone, hit record, and slide it under the sofa.

"Guys, we're not going anywhere, okay?" I said, standing up. "We'll be here when Ms. Alexandra is finished."

They both nodded. Alexandra smiled and turned her attention to Robbie:

"I hear you're quite the baseball player."

When Allison and I stepped from the room, I walked past her and made my way downstairs. Janice was in the kitchen reading a romance novel and humming to herself. I found a spot on the couch in the living room where a fire had been burning. Picking up my latest issue of *Rolling Stone*, I flipped through its pages for the next ten minutes or so. By the time the upstairs door had opened and footsteps were descending the stairs, I had come close to convincing myself that I was spending another relaxing evening at home with my family.

"I enjoyed meeting you all," Alexandra said, extending her hand to each of us.

The poor woman. The only fitting exit strategy would have been to snap her fingers before vanishing into a vaporous cloud. When the kids were no longer within earshot, she told us she would conclude her investigation within forty-five days. Allison said nothing. I nodded and thanked Alexandra for coming. She walked out into the cold night air and got into her car she had parked on the street. Standing on my front porch for a few moments, I watched as she sat idly while the engine warmed. After a few moments, I closed the door and ran upstairs to retrieve and listen to the conversation I had recorded on my iPhone.

Alexandra was clearly good at her job. She first ingratiated herself to my kids. Not terribly difficult to do with a three and seven-year-old, but she was nevertheless skilled at talking with them. She brought up toys and TV shows and asked about their favorite foods. Their answers belied the notion that this was a stranger speaking with them. On the contrary, they generated the kind of enthusiasm reserved for some favorite auntie. Before long, she moved on to weightier matters. Whether they have their school friends over. Whether meals are served and shared regularly. How Mom and Dad interact with them. How Mom and Dad treat one another.

The dialogue seemed pretty standard. Nothing revelatory. It was evident that the kids were not damaged. Not yet anyway. When I looked out the window of my bedroom, I saw that Alexandra was still sitting in her car. It must have been sufficiently warm by that point. I imagined her to either be jotting down a few notes or making a phone call. Watching her for another minute filled me with the temptation to grab my kids and bound out into the street and ask her if she had room for the three of us, to tell her that we were easy and fun-loving and were willing to go *any*where.

•   •   •   •   •

As the days wore on, conversations between Allison and I were starting to become redundant. She continued to plead her contrition, stating how she loved me and our family and our life together and how she would do anything to make amends. It was a lapse in judgment, she said, and she never meant to deliberately hurt me or our children. She bawled and begged and worked tirelessly to make me see how she was human and had simply lost herself for a bit, but had to hit rock bottom to once again be found.

"You've been *found* for the same reason anyone claims they're *found*," I said. "Because you got *caught*. That's all. You would've kept it going. Your little threesome. You would've taken it to the next level. Upped the ante. Using my imagination over what exactly that means sickens me."

"No," she protested, "I swear. I swear I love you. I never meant to hurt you or the kids. I just got caught up in something these past months."

I pointed out what we had both known before her secrets were revealed: that what she had been caught up in, vanity, shallowness, self-absorption, technology, was more or less the bane of her existence for *years*, not months.

"I tried to save you from yourself," I said.

"I know."

"I did. I tried to save you from yourself."

"I know you did."

"I don't care how that sounds, either: arrogant or preachy or condescending. Because it's true. I did. I tried to save you from yourself."

"I know."

It was true. I had tried, for years, to be the catalyst for some type of self-awareness on her part. To make her see how her behaviors - the selfishness, the materialism, the narcissism - was affecting our family. More often than not, I was accused of being too judgmental, overly critical, a nag, a control freak. Yet I had control over not one facet of the marriage. The fact of the matter is that this was a woman who listened to not a single word I ever had to say. I would half joke with my father that Allison had turned me into Fredo from *The Godfather*. Fredo, played by the late John Cazale, is the epitome of a milquetoast – especially where his oversexed flake of a wife is concerned. This is cemented in Part II during the Lake Tahoe party scene where she's inebriated and falling down on the dance floor. After an unsuccessful attempt at admonishing her, Fredo skulks over to his younger brother, Pacino's Michael, and says, emasculated and dispirited, "I can't control 'er, Mikey."

The time came to examine the legal side of the matter. This seemed imminent. Many discussions were had with my family over the various implications Allison's behavior would have on my future. There was my job to consider. And my financial well-being. My standing in the community. And most importantly, my ability to parent my children in a safe, healthy environment. Remaining married to someone who would likely become an ex-convict, a registered sex offender, a pariah in the community, a financial and legal liability, would put all of this into serious jeopardy. The matter of love and affection seemed not at all considerations I could tamper with. Besides, love and affection were near casualties, writhing under the recent deluge of my wife's abhorrent misdeeds.

Ray Hassett, the attorney my mother mentioned at the bagel place, has an established and well-respected practice out of Glastonbury; he came to me through my sister's old friend and college roommate, an attorney herself. She not only interned with Ray, singing his praises in terms of both professionalism and bedside manner, but had hired him to oversee her own recent divorce. With my mother and sister in tow, I met with Ray for a consultation.

Hillary, Ray's paralegal, ushered us into his conference room where we sat around a massive oblong wooden table. She brought in some bottled water and stayed for a moment, making small talk about the weather. After a moment, Ray entered. At over six feet tall, with a broad build and a trim, grayish goatee, he shook our hands before taking a seat at the head of the table.

"Looks like we got one hell of a situation here," he said. "I know the general facts from what I've read about the case, but why don't you take me through it."

I told him about my January 7th meeting in T.J.'s office with the Madison Police. I talked about the accusations against my wife, as well as her duplicitous behavior during the last year. Ray took notes on a white legal pad, looking up every so often to nod or shake his head in disbelief.

"Take me through the marriage," he said. "Was it stable? Any abuse? Drinking? Tell me how you two met. Tell me about your kids, your jobs, your life together."

Ray had an easy way about him. He was a good listener and not at all pushy or patronizing. When he had the information he needed, he began to lay out my options. He talked about assets and the house and custody. My mother and sister chimed in:

"Rob *has* to get full custody," they said in near unison. "What are the chances of that?"

Ray sighed. Then he played with his goatee for a bit before consulting the notes in front of him.

"It's difficult," he said. "Not impossible. But difficult."

He went on to talk about various statutes and precedents, which I found uninteresting; I was hanging onto the one word he had said earlier: *difficult.* By the time he finished explaining the custodial challenges that lay ahead, I mentioned again that I could not be without my children for any length of time.

"I understand," he said, offering nothing more.

My dealings with lawyers were limited, and my impression of them vacillated between two extremes: Atticus Finch from *To Kill a Mockingbird* and Dr. Gonzo from *Fear and Loathing in Las Vegas.* Rectitude versus depravity. My expectations were thus ambiguous. But one bothersome fact remained: Ray was circumspect about custody.

Joseph Garr out of Seymour, a rural wasteland just north of New Haven, seemed to have no such reservations. From the onset, despite looking like some weathered insurance salesman with his discolored teeth, thinning black hair, and slight paunch, Garr exuded a sleek and even imperious demeanor, speaking slowly yet forcefully, pausing in his speech to take stock of his wit and insight, and moving with the deliberateness of a sultan on the verge of some life-altering pilgrimage. His professional reputation was that of a hardcore litigator, something I continued to remind myself of as I sat in his cramped and cluttered office, my father and stepmother seated next to me.

"Start from the beginning," he said, breaking out a leather notebook and ballpoint pen. "Your marriage. I want the good, the bad, the ugly. I want to know how you met. How you spent your time together and apart. What life was like before children. After children. Did drugs and alcohol ever enter the picture?"

Like I had done with Ray just two days before, I opened up and shared with this stranger the details of my marital life. Yet unlike Ray, Garr seemed interested only as far as the stories pertained to my case. There was no human touch. I could have told him that my wife made me watch while she had sex with strange men she picked up at convenience stores, and his response would have been to nod his head, take a few notes, and move to the next question. My father and stepmother said little. They only chimed in when the matter of custody came up.

"We'll get him full custody," Garr said, looking their way. "And we'll get him the house, too."

His confidence was understated when he said this, like a veteran athlete speaking at a press conference and promising victory because he knows too well every possible strategy of his opponent. My father and I glanced at one another, tacitly sharing in the wonderful potential of Garr's revelation.

"Why don't you take some time," Garr said, looking in my direction, "and think about what you'd like to do. But I'll be honest with you: The sooner the better. Time is of the essence."

I nodded, waiting for a further explanation. He offered nothing. My father asked about a good diner in the area where we might discuss the matter. Garr directed us to a favorite spot of his down the street. He shook our hands and said he hoped to see us soon.

"Full custody," I said over a spinach and tomato omelet at a place called The Sandwich Man Family Restaurant. "What do you guys think?"

"I think you need to be as certain about this as you've ever been about anything," Helene said.

My father nodded in agreement with his wife. He had been pretty well impaired by what had happened to my family. He wasn't cut out for conflict in the best of times. A proponent of simplicity – simplicity in discourse, in relationships, in lifestyle – any obfuscating factors were not only maddening to him, but as abstract as though they were conceived by some black magic ritual. He was prepared to *listen* to options, but not necessarily originate any of his own. I was fine with this.

"How can I move forward with her?" I said. "It's impossible after what she's done. Imagine the kind of life it would be."

I had to let the practical side of my brain trample the romantic side; this meant unfurling banners that read IRREVERSIBLE TRAGEDY – GET OUT NOW.

"She didn't give you a choice," Helene said, "and that might have been deliberate on her part – to destroy any chance of putting it back together."

This was a theory of my stepmother's I had heard on numerous occasions in the last couple of weeks. It went something like this: Allison hated me. It was a hate born out of jealousy that had spread like a virus over the past few years. Jealousy that I was mostly happy in my life. I was a natural parent, having established wonderful relationships with my children, relationships born out of respect, affection, and the investment of time. I had good friends, a band, a burgeoning writing career, a recent promotion at work, and family in the area. She, meanwhile, had become consumed with only herself. This meant obsessive fitness routines. An obstinance towards growing older. Looking to others for her self-worth. And while brooding in her resentment towards me, she managed to convince herself that she was somehow a victim of circumstance and neglect, rather than simply a wife and mother and teacher.

"This is not going to be cheap," my father pointed out.

He went on to talk a bit about money. Folding some of my omelet into a piece of toast before taking a bite, I half listened. I had only a few thousand dollars to my name and was no doubt going to need help. Yet the last thing I wanted was to acknowledge and discuss it. The entire affair had emasculated me enough. Now I was to be financially indebted to my family?

"You need to call your mother and see if she'll pay half the retainer," my father said.

Excusing myself from the table, I made the call then and there. My mother asked about Garr, his predictions, his temperament. I told her I liked Ray better, but that Garr was confident over the matter of custody. She paused.

"Then I guess we'd better go with him," she said. "I'll mail you the five thousand today."

We drove back to Garr's office in silence. The weight of what I was to embark upon was settling upon me. After telling him that we wished to move forward with the divorce, Garr's manner changed immediately. He was at once warm and avuncular, extending his hand and declaring that he was *proud* of me. My stomach dropped. Helene handed him the check and he wasted no time in snatching it from her and sliding it into his breast pocket. He was grinning like a man who had followed a winning tip at the racetrack. The avarice was unsettling. I told myself it was his very shrewdness that might get me what I was after in the divorce. Yet I couldn't help thinking, as we left his office and walked outside into the raw, whipping cold, that Garr was not at all the right man for the job.

•   •   •   •   •

The next several days brought with them many questions. Would I be able to force Allison into vacating the house? Should I begin dividing our assets? Reroute my paycheck? Each time I called Garr's office, he wasn't in. I left messages with his secretary, who promised he would call me back. Sometimes he would. Often he would not. When he did, he would tell me to hold tight and that he would soon be in touch.

"Is there anything I should do in the meantime?"

"Keep a journal of what transpires between the two of you," he said. "And record your conversations."

"What for?"

"They might prove useful."

So I got to work on a journal, documenting pivotal talks we had since January 7th. Talks about her indiscretions and her past and our marriage and her mental illness. And I began carrying a small handheld tape recorder around the house. Concealing it in my sweatshirt or pants pocket, I had perfected the act of pressing *play* at a moment's notice. But the conversations were redundant and not at all revealing. Mostly they were desperate pleas for me to not leave her. Many were filled with tears and declarations of love. There were even a few pseudo-intellectual stabs at equivocation. Then, on January 19th, at 7:49 p.m., we engaged in a conversation that would prove to be far more salient.

I was holed up in the master bedroom, draped in my comforter, watching a reenactment of the Hoover Dam being constructed, when Allison asked to speak with me. I kept my eyes on the TV and felt around for the tape recorder.

"How are you doing?" she asked.

It was too absurd to even answer.

"Can we talk for a minute?" she said.

I found the proper button and pressed it. Then, with a heavy sigh, I paused the TV and listened to what she had to say. She stated how she was floored that she could make the decision she had made when she loved me and our children. She couldn't understand it, she said over and over. She acknowledged that I was good to her, good to our children, a good man – not abusive or violent or unstable in any way. I was undeserving of what had happened, she acknowledged.

"It was just a bad decision," she said.

I was maddened by her continued use of that word: decision.

"Did you say *decision?*" I said, looking up at her. "As in *singular?*"

She said nothing. I explained that right then and there she was forbidden from ever referring to this matter as a single act. I pointed out that her actions – the scouting, the preying, the enticing, the molesting – lasted nearly a year. She didn't argue. Then I asked her to take me through the chronology of events spanning back to the previous spring. She did so, willingly. And lucidly.

She talked about having profound feelings for fourteen-year-old Gabe. How she texted him constantly. Texts mostly of a sexual nature, propositioning Gabe and inquiring about his sexual experiences. I was careful to guide the trajectory of events so she didn't leave any gaps. Which she did not. She was seamless in her acknowledgments. Her voice and manner were so steady that it was unnerving. She might as well have been reminiscing about some European odyssey she took when she was a college student.

The story then took a detour into her exploits with Zach, victim #2. Her gym buddy. They began talking after Gabe lost interest. She sent Zach nude selfies. He paid her two separate visits to her classroom. She made it very worth his while. And sealed her fate in the process.

"So you see," I said, "you don't have the right to call it a *mistake* or a *decision*. You made a *series* of awful decisions over a ten-month period. You could have – and should have – stopped yourself on numerous occasions. But you didn't. And now…"

This ended the conversation. There was nothing left for either of us to say. Defeated, Allison nodded her head and started to walk away. She stopped herself when she was just a foot or two from the door. Then she turned to me and asked if we could share the bed that night. Hurling an awestruck glance into space, I aimed the remote towards the TV and pressed play. When she left the room, I shut the tape recorder off and hid it under the mattress.

•   •   •   •   •

One of the few times Garr called was to inform me that he had finalized the divorce papers.

"She's ready to be served," he told me one afternoon in late January.

"Should I tell her it's coming?"

"That's up to you."

"Any benefits either way?"

"The element of surprise is always good. But then again, you don't want her to go nuts and cause a scene in front of your kids."

Garr added that he still needed to coordinate the date and time with the state marshal who would be delivering her the summons.

"Could take a few days," he said.

He advised me to suggest to Allison the idea of mediation. This was, through a neutral third party, the simplest and most cost effective means of dissolving the marriage. I knew she would never go for it. I told this to Garr.

"Then we'll have to see how things play out," he said before hanging up.

Two days later, when the kids were asleep and Janice was watching TV, I found my wife washing up in the bathroom. The time had arrived to break the news. I was hopeful it would cause her to move out of the house.

"It's too soon," she cried. "Please don't do this. Please. Come to therapy with me. This is worth saving. I'll do anything. I'll go to therapy for the rest of my life. You can come *with* me. We can find out together why I did this to our family."

The mere suggestion of couples counseling seemed to me the pinnacle of her narcissism. I wasn't about to let her get away with it.

"You're so interesting to yourself, aren't you?" I said. "Not to me. Wanna expedite the therapeutic process? Here goes: Wanna know the cause of your catastrophe? You're shallow, vain, self-absorbed, weak, and pathetic. There you are. One session. One *sentence*, even. Five seconds. Free of charge."

I had become quite adept at being a cruel son-of-a-bitch. It was hardly cathartic. Often, by the time the last caustic syllable was launched from my tongue, I was full of as much self-loathing as I was contempt for her. She pleaded with me some more that it was too soon to file for divorce. There was a part of me that agreed with this. We were far from being unfettered newlyweds. We had cultivated a life together. Twelve years of marriage. Two perfect children. A lovely home. And, the occasional happiness and hardship that came with it all.

"Just do yourself a favor," I said. "When you get the papers, call the law office of Joseph Garr and inquire about mediation. It's the most civil and cost-effective way out of this – whatever the hell *this* has now become."

As if sensing that he was being summoned, Garr called within the next hour, advising me to turn her taped confession over to the cops.

"Now's a good time," he said, not explaining any further.

"What do I do? Drive to the police station, introduce myself, and play the tape for them?"

"That's exactly what you do."

"What will they do with it?"

"Decide on its value. Maybe turn it over to the prosecution. Maybe disregard it completely."

This was one hell of a development. The tape was a comfort up until this point. Nothing more. I knew it had the potential to incite some action, yet I never figured it would be put to use. I called my mother and talked it over with her.

"If he's advising you to do it, you should listen."

"I can't believe it's as simple as that."

"Given all these complications, take simplicity when you can get it."

As I drove to the Madison Police station, I imagined the conversation I'd likely have with my children in ten years, and then again in twenty, and every so often after that. It would be dense with defensiveness and sad resignation and perplexed expressions that would see our faces contort just enough to suggest an attempt at reconciling with such an otherworldly past.

When I arrived at the station, I asked to speak with the detective who was handling the Allison Marchese investigation. After a moment, the stocky, baby-faced officer I had seen back on January 7th at DHHS emerged and led me into a room the size of a walk-in closet. The only furnishings were a small desk and two wooden chairs.

"I need to inform you that this interview is being filmed," he said, inviting me to sit down.

I told him my purpose in being there. He asked to hear the tape. I produced the recorder from my coat pocket and played it for him. His pensiveness over the tape's content told me he was pleased. He asked to hear it a second time.

"I don't feel great about doing this," I pointed out. "But my lawyer..."

Cutting me off, he said I was doing the right thing. He added that even *he* didn't know if the tape was admissible evidence. Still, I felt sick over my presence there, sick over the content of the tape, over how things had turned out, and how they would likely end up for my family.

"My children," I said to the detective.

I never finished the sentence. I didn't have to. Nodding his head, he seemed to grasp my meaning.

Calling Garr on my way home that evening, I told him about my meeting with the police. He assured me it was a worthy insurance policy.

"It's the closest you can come to protecting yourself and your kids right now," he said.

This marked one of the few times he mentioned Robbie and Riley.

"I understand," I said, not knowing if I really did. "What now?"

"We wait," he said. "We wait for her to be served."

And so she was. On January 30th. Garr called me at work to let me know.

"Okay," I said, "what does this mean?"

"It means the wheels are in motion."

"What now?"

"Let's see how she reacts."

Like a shrewd CEO of some tenuous fortune 500 company. That's how. No histrionics. No more pleading. Nothing. In fact, there was a metamorphosis. I detected, for the first time since the incident broke, an attitude, an edge, an indignation even. She seemed emboldened. Ready to fight.

I broke the news of the divorce to my son that very evening. After our bedtime routine, I laid down with him and held his face close to mine and told him that I loved him, that his mother loved him, that he was perfect, and that he would always be my boy, and that I was sorry. I said this last part over and over again:

"I'm sorry. I'm sorry. I'm sorry I could only give you seven years of this life. I did my best."

Then I revealed that me and his mother had decided to no longer be friends. This was familiar phrasing I knew he would understand. I had used those very words to depict the division that had claimed his Papa and Mimi decades earlier. He began to cry. So I held him tighter.

"Why?" he asked through his tears.

"Because Mommy broke my heart."

This was a visceral response. If I had time to think on it, I would have said something less confusing.

"Can she make it up to you?"

A genius question. Precocious as hell. I could think of nothing more heartbreaking or devastating or full of earnest daydreamy optimism. All I could do is lay there with him, which I did until he was sleepy. Then I kissed him goodnight and made my way downstairs where Allison and Janice were watching *Downton Abbey*.

"Can I see you for a minute?" I said to my wife.

She and her mother shared a look. This was the first time in weeks I had initiated a conversation. I can only imagine what they thought I might be up to. Janice paused the TV, and Allison and I went upstairs to talk.

"I just told Robbie," I said. "Which marked the single worst moment of my life. It was beyond description. And I just want you to know that whatever anger I felt for you before just multiplied by a thousand. It's official now, if it wasn't before, that I will never forgive you for what you've done."

She began to tear up. I stared at her. After a moment, Janice made her way up the stairs.

"I'll tell Riley tomorrow," I said. "I can only handle one heartache at a time."

Janice, shooting me a derisive look, made her way towards Allison and steered her away from me.

"Do you have something to say, Janice?" I said.

"Not to you I don't."

"Yeah. Brilliant. Go watch your fucking soap opera, the two of you. You're perfect for each other."

•   •   •   •   •

The following morning was a Saturday. I imagined the kind of sleep Allison had the evening before, or what she might have dreamed of – survival, restoration, reincarnation. Either way, she woke with an air of stolidness about her. It was as if she had waded through an impossible obstacle course, one with unprecedented perils, defying all odds, and now held firmly in her grasp a casual indifference towards challenge and suffering.

Once she showered and dressed, she told me she and her mother would be taking the kids to a movie and then to Mystic Aquarium.

"We'd love for you to join us."

I shook my head at her invite and mentioned how she didn't appear to grasp our redefined roles to one another. Then I asked a question I had already brought up a few times:

"Is there a chance of you moving out anytime soon?"

"Nope."

"You really are living in some type of fantasy world."

"Well, I'll be living it right here."

I vacillated between awe and disdain. We were now starring in one of Woody Allen's lesser known films, the tragicomedy where pain and pathos battle it out amidst self-righteous quips and passive little smirks. It's the land of unfulfillment. It's where no one wins. And as fate would have it, I was due to play the loser role like I had never played it before.

Dear Divorce,

You're an embarrassment. You're failure and finality. You're downsized living spaces, pre-packaged dinners, new financial hardships. You're like a low income housing project. Or cancer. Or Walmart. Your pernicious influence wreaks havoc on societies. You're a dirty word that has become too tolerated, too mainstream, too matter-of-fact. And your stats are boastful and obnoxious.

We knew each other when I was much younger. Eighteen-years-old to be exact. And I hated you then. You threw everything of mine into the fire and hid every water source within reach. You caused heart palpitations. You thrived on being some sort of bloated monster to all of us who were forced to look you in the eyes. You had tremendous influence over me – and you knew this – and you got off on how far reaching that influence was. You're a pimp, a pusher. You're as unmoving and unyielding as the darkness in which you deal. And there's not a speck of light to be found within a million miles of where you reside.

Your biggest advantage is your unwieldiness. No one knows how to handle you. Or react to your presence, which is so often furtive to the point of being abusive. So people act out and make poor decisions. Sometimes fatal ones. But you don't give a shit. You just keep your perfect posture intact and take it all in, knowing full well you have the upper hand, and you always will.

I know my metaphors are mixed. All over the place, in fact. They have to be, I suppose, but not because you're at all hard to define. You're not. It's because I have a hundred ways to hate you. Probably more, in fact, you funereal fucker.

Case in point: You've met my children. You swooped down on them while they slept and played and been oblivious in their delicious innocence. This alone makes me want to bludgeon you with the thick steel of a double barrel shotgun before turning it on you and bringing you to your knees before blasting you into oblivion. Too much? Maybe. Yet please don't mistake this for tough-guy talk. It's not. I'm aware of the notion that you have shackled yourself to the two most precious people in my life. I'm also aware of the notion that you will put on a pretense that you are not attempting to submerge them into the doldrums of a subpar life; you will instead posit that they will merely have some challenges ahead and some character building opportunities. But you and I both know you are looking for casualties. Especially given these very fucked up circumstances. But you will not find casualties in my children. Still, do whatever you think you need to do to fulfill your purpose. It hardly matters. Because I will be there every second of every day. And I will be watching so closely and intently that my breath and yours will at times become one. And my children will feel them both. And they will be confused on occasion. But I will be there to explain it to them. *And we will one day mock you. And laugh like idiots. Happy idiots.*

Time will move on. And my presence will have only grown stronger. My children will have also grown stronger. And we will continue to laugh. And the laughter will piss you off. Because it will be real laughter. You will recognize this. By then we will not even attempt to cut you loose. Because by then it will not matter. You will be dead, worthless weight. A battle scar they will look at from time to time. Nothing more.

I suppose I've been pretty long winded. I suppose some might even consider this letter nothing more than an angry, arrogant rant. And I suppose I could have been a bit more succinct by just stating the obvious – that this is a competition between me and you. A battle, even. And one involving power and hubris. I suppose, then, that the entire affair can be reduced to a simple challenge between old acquaintances. As if you didn't know, I gladly accept.

Disrespectfully,
Rob

Chapter 3

With my children on their way to Mystic Aquarium with Allison and her mother, I welcomed the opportunity for some alone time. My daily routine had been the same since my wife's crimes were revealed on January 7th. I went to work every day, teaching literature and creative writing to my juniors and seniors while facing a maelstrom of pity as I tried to maintain some dignity. I played with my children, bittersweet though the time was. I ate and slept as best I could. I rehearsed with my band. But solitude was as foreign to me as inner peace. I was lonely as hell, but rarely alone.

Not to mention I wanted some time to survey my home. Allison had free reign of the place all day, Monday through Friday, and it became customary for me to come home from work and find my closet door ajar or my dresser drawers slightly messier than how I had left them. God knows what she thought I had secretly stashed, but she underestimated me if she thought I would leave behind anything of value. The truth is that on January 9th, two days after her betrayal broke, I collected what little cash was in the house, a handful of valuable baseball cards, and perhaps the most important items: my kids' passports. I had recently conjured images of Allison stealing Robbie and Riley while I was at work and then making her way to the Canadian border just north of Houlton. I envisioned a high-speed chase and border patrol and even helicopters. Then I would scoff at the notion and tell myself there was no way she was brazen enough for such a stunt. Then, just as quickly, I would remind myself that I truly didn't know what she was capable of.

As I walked around my house, I recall being struck by how different it suddenly appeared. It was a bright day and the cheerful sunlight fought to devour the gloom that ran in circles from floor to ceiling. I loved my home from the moment we had moved in a few years earlier. Now something about it had changed. It was impossible to describe. Every home has an energy, a personality, and when both are compromised with sudden shocking sadness, the walls no longer speak in memories, but in blunted silence and foreign looking facades. I knew in that moment, walking around my house, that I would never again get it back.

It seemed like a perfect time for the errand I had been planning for a few days. So I got in my car and drove to Clinton, two miles up the street, to pay a visit to someone I had been talking to on and off for the past week. She wasn't expecting me, so it was a short visit at her salon. We made plans to talk later that day and to even get together in the upcoming weeks. It was all I needed to head back home to get some songwriting done. I sat down at my desk in my home office and began to fool with a tune I had been stuck on for a few days. I remember being frustrated over the lack of inspiration. Arrogantly, I somehow figured that my brain would be a wellspring of free-flowing lines like what was produced on Dylan's *Blood on the Tracks*, the preeminent divorce record. What I had instead was something much simpler, a tune called "The Damage Done." At that point, I had only a single verse:

Dreams fall from my head as I sleep
Tears fall from my eyes as I weep
Over damage done
I promised to write a song for you
Maybe a murder ballad or two
Over damage done

Strumming the tune's melody on my guitar, waiting for more words to come, I suddenly noticed the black box on my desk. I had forgotten all about it during the past few weeks. I set the guitar down and picked up the box. Not at all surprised to find it empty, I let it fall to the floor while cursing myself. So stupid. It wasn't so much the missing Amazon gift cards I had recently received for my fortieth birthday, but more who gave them to me. My sister, Amy.

My relationship with my sister had long been a complicated one. Often relegated as pawns throughout our parents' divorce decades earlier, as well as in their long-standing and mutual hatred of one another, Amy and I vacillated in our allegiances and tolerances. This, naturally, took its toll over the years. But we somehow managed to come through it all with a sense of bitter jocularity, commiserating over injustices heaped upon us by our sometimes feckless parents.

Her recent support over my troubles was nearly staggering. Some fierce and hitherto dormant sisterly instinct rose up in her like floodwater. Instincts that had her calling me every day, offering financial and emotional support I most definitely needed, looking after my children on occasion, and sharing in my unbelievable sorrow over what had happened to my family. I remember feeling like we were kids once again, vulnerable over the demise of our own domestic equilibrium, reeling from the tumult and shock caused by our own parents' misdeeds.

The missing Amazon cards thus struck me in an especially profound way. It was an affront to my sister and her love for me and our past together. I wanted those fucking gift cards back. So I sat around the house and waited for Allison to return from her outing with our children. My plan was to confront her, explaining the emotional gravity of what she had so obviously stolen. Yet in just under ten minutes, that plan went entirely to hell. She was barely through the door when I approached her.

"I have no idea what you're talking about," she said.

"Oh no?"

My mother-in-law, feigning oblivion over the matter, retreated to the family room and began to read. Following Allison upstairs, I persisted over the stolen cards.

"Spare me your lies," I said, "and give me back the goddamn cards."

Her denial masqueraded behind acts of subterfuge like cleaning the bathroom and hanging a sweater in the closet. Securing my children in their room, and instructing that they play, I refused to drop the matter. She maintained her innocence. My patience began to wane. The stand-off soon escalated into a hostage negotiation. The conditions were that I return an item she claimed was missing – she accused me of making off with a pair of small studded diamond earrings – and she might suddenly remember the whereabouts of my gift cards. Fed up, I made my way downstairs and swiped her purse from the kitchen counter. Then, because I wished for some theatrics, some mild spectacle, I raced up the stairs and emptied the purse on the floor in front of her. Allison merely watched as I made a fool out of myself, tossing receipts and chapsticks and loose change this way and that; within seconds, it was evident that what I was looking for was nowhere to be found.

Before this thought was given space to breath, I heard the dialing of a phone. When I looked up, she was speaking to a 911 operator, telling them I had thrown her to the ground and pulled her hair. In an instant, I grabbed the phone from her.

"Ma'am, she's lying," I said, "I never touched her."

"Sir, go into another room and lock the door," the dispatcher stated calmly.

"I'm going into the bathroom," I said.

"Be sure to lock the door. Police officers are enroute."

"It's locked."

I could hear my children in the next room. They had heard the commotion and rushed to see what was happening.

"Sir, are you there?"

"I'm here."

"Good. Just stay put."

"I'm assuming you know who my wife is and what she's recently done to disgrace our family."

"Just stay put, sir. The police will be there shortly."

I kept talking. I couldn't help myself. It's pathetic to admit it, but I wanted an ally in this nameless, faceless stranger.

"Her life is pretty much over, so she wants to destroy mine," I said. "More so than she's already done."

"Please just keep calm, sir."

Thoughts of Robbie and Riley suddenly filled my head. In minutes, they would have to witness the presence of police officers in their home, storming up and down the stairs in heavy black shoes, questioning

Mommy and Daddy, radioing the precinct, and babbling their cryptic cop jargon.

"I need to get my kids."

"Please stay put, sir."

Ignoring her, I opened the door and coaxed Robbie and Riley into the bathroom with me. Allison was now hysterical and talking to her mother, who at this point must have longed to be back in Canada.

"It's okay, guys, let's just hang out in here for a bit. Nothing to worry about."

I pressed the mute button on the phone.

"What happened?" Robbie asked.

"Nothing, buddy, it's all good. Just hang out with Daddy in here for a few minutes."

The dispatcher grew a little frantic.

"Sir, why are you muting the phone? Are you still there?"

"Why is Mommy crying?" Riley asked.

"She's just a little sad, baby."

"Should we see if she's okay?" Robbie asked.

"Sir, are you still isolated from your wife?"

Unmuting the phone, I told her I was and that everything was fine. Then I muted it again.

"Daddy, should we see if Mommy's okay?"

Looking down at my seven-year-old boy, I was taken with his magnanimous curiosity over his mother's welfare.

"Sure, buddy, go see if she's okay. Both of you go."

"Sir, *why* are you muting the phone?"

"I'm not. I'm here."

Opening the door, I released my children to their mother. They remained at her side for the next few minutes until four policers arrived at our house. They of course knew the Marchese's as of late and must have expected to see the worst: a murder/suicide, maybe an armed standoff, or perhaps a histrionic female with torn clothing, fresh blood and bruises on her face, and a vivid tale to tell. They saw nothing of the kind. What they saw were the contents of an overturned purse on the bedroom floor. And they saw me, calm and convivial, inviting them into my home, cooperating and offering a lucid explanation about a woman on the brink of losing her mind with embarrassment and indignation over being caught having affairs with multiple teenage boys.

They also saw two beautiful, young children who moved nervously from room to room, stunned to find so many armed mythic figures tramp through their house. As for Allison, she was crying and carrying on, huddling miserably with her mother, and declaring that she could no longer live this way. Scoffing over her theatrics, I made a comment that I thought was as apropos as it was amusing. The Madison Police appeared to disagree with me.

"Sir, move into the next room," one of the officers said.

"Why?"

"Just do it."

I did as he told me.

"Ma'am, please take the children upstairs."

Within seconds, Allison and Janice were escorting Robbie and Riley to their rooms. I was left alone, quite certain as to what was about to happen. Within moments, I was surrounded by three of the cops and told to put my hands behind my back.

It bothers me to say this, but I must: The arresting officer was an asshole. It would have been better if he wasn't. It would give the story a pinch of irony, which is always a useful narrative spice. I wish I could say that he and I saw eye to eye on the Red Sox or muscle cars, or something, that we bullshitted for a bit before his legal obligations took hold. It would be poetic to declare that I know it broke his heart to slap those cuffs on me while my two children waited upstairs, uncertain what was happening and why their home had been overtaken by law enforcement. On the contrary, Officer French rather enjoyed his errand that late afternoon on January 31st. I know he did.

"Sir, what exactly is the charge?" I asked, waiting to be read my rights.

He told me to call him Frenchie before he called the station to let them know he was making the arrest. What a collar this will surely be, I thought to myself: the husband of the most notorious woman in town. At the very least, I convinced myself, he'll be embarrassed when he finds out my relationship with the Madison Police Department. We'll straighten it all out once we arrive at the station. Just a minor snag, I thought.

"Sir, can you please explain the charge?"

"Frenchie."

"Frenchie, can you please explain the charge?"

He and two other officers led me to the foyer closet where they let me slide my feet into my sneakers. The fourth officer went upstairs to let my wife and mother-in-law know I was being removed from the house. Imagining their reactions sickened me. No doubt they would feel that justice was being served, that a tremendous burden was lifted, that they were now out of harm's way.

"Disorderly conduct," Officer French told me matter-of-factly. "And interfering with a 911 call."

"For real?" I asked.

"Let's go," he said, neglecting to read me my rights as he led me out into the cold January air.

The last few moments of daylight were looming. The sky had grown somber and was crisscrossed with streaks of cheerless looking clouds. My suburban neighborhood, called The Highlands, is so often quiet and vacant. Even on a bright sunshine-filled day, people sightings are rare. This has always bewildered me, as the houses, all lovely, well-built Capes and Colonials with meticulous gardens, are huddled incredibly close together. I was thankful that this particular January evening saw no onlookers rubbernecking in the streets or in their driveways. Yet I suppose it's quite possible, and likely probable, that they had cushier vantage points from the warm comfort of their homes.

"Can you explain the disorderly conduct charge?" I asked once Frenchie stuffed me in the rear of his cruiser with my hands still cuffed behind my back.

He ignored me, calling the station again to let them know we were enroute.

"Sir. Frenchie."

"It was the ugly comment you made," he said. "It only escalated the matter."

I needed a minute to recall what I had said just moments ago. Suddenly it hit me. Unbelievable. I was in absolute disbelief. What about First Amendment rights? Wasn't this America? I felt the sanctimoniousness creeping in. Beyond absurd, I thought, to be arrested for referring to my wife as the "blow job queen of Madison."

"That's what did it, huh?" I said.

"That's what did it."

"Well then," I said, "I guess her mouth and mine are the things that got us each into trouble."

Frenchie took the scenic route out of my neighborhood, driving past no fewer than the houses of three students I was currently teaching at Daniel Hand High School.

"Will I be able to talk to Detective M. when we arrive at the station?" I asked.

"Not sure if he's there."

"I'd really like to talk to him. I think he might vouch for me. You see, I just recently met with him."

Officer Frenchie looked at me in his rearview mirror.

"I helped him out," I said. "In his investigation – against my wife."

"I see."

"So I'd really like to speak with him."

"Not sure if he's there."

"I gave him a tape."

"A tape?"

"A tape. My lawyer advised me to cooperate in the investigation against my wife. So that's what I did."

"I see."

"It's a confession. *Her* confession. It's going to help me get custody of my children."

The time seemed appropriate to use this information. After all, it was weighty information. Leverage, in fact. That's what it was: leverage. If I had contemplated this notion for a minute, it would have dawned on me that I was now superfluous to the MPD. They had what they wanted from me, so why would they see their way to striking some kind of deal. Officer Frenchie, now deft in his ability to dash my optimism, dismissed my implied agenda:

"You're *getting* arrested," he said, "despite who you speak with once we arrive at the station."

"Of course," I muttered, now imagining the talk I would soon have with my parents.

Not to mention my lawyer. I'd have to call him once I was booked. That, I knew, would be one hell of a conversation. Garr, when he could actually find the time to meet, filled our minutes with condescension, lectures, and warnings about upcoming payments that would soon be due. He was on retainer for a mere couple of weeks and he blew through money like a degenerate gambler.

I came to dread communicating with him. His insouciance over my ordeal was maddening. Whenever he spoke, he had an air of aloofness about him, as though he was stuck in a perpetual daydream. Never once did he ask how I was doing on an emotional level. More importantly, he never asked about Robbie and Riley. I'll concede that I must have been a pain in the ass as a client. My anxiety and impatience, hastened by my recent devastation, knew no limits. It was therefore rare that I would keep my mouth shut. Custody, the house, my finances, the future, the fate of my soon to be ex-wife. The questions were ceaseless.

"Are you listening to me?" Garr would ask.

"Yes."

"No you're not."

"I am."

"You're not. You're not at all. You're not understanding. We get through A first before we move on to B."

"Okay, but..."

"We get through A *first* before we move on to B."

"I understand, but..."

"You so clearly do *not* understand."

The Madison Police Station is located on the town campus, directly across from Central Office, the public school's administrative buildings – in other words, where my bosses work. Another unpleasant phone call would have to be made. As the cruiser pulled around the station and into the sally port, I remember thinking that my life was turning into a Paul Thomas Anderson film. Anderson, known for *Magnolia* and *There Will Be Blood*, infuses into his movies the kind of despair that becomes so heavy that it eventually gives way to a kind of cathartic black humor.

His protagonists are so often mired in an almost savage sort of existential crises that the direness of their dilemma can turn biblical. His shots are long and unsettling and offer panoramic views of anguish in its rawest incarnation. I might as well have been Don Cheadle in *Boogie Nights* or Adam Sandler in *Punch Drunk Love*, desperate and frustrated, sucked into a hideous vacuum of violence and other-worldly humiliation, alone, and contemplating a numbing pain with only a dumbfounded expression on my pathetic face.

Of course I didn't shut up during the time it took to take my mugshots and fingerprints. I continued the trend of laying out my respectful diatribe over the injustice of it all.

"I just don't understand the legality of this," I said. "I'm being arrested for being a smartass?"

"You're being arrested for disorderly conduct and interfering with a 911 call."

"If taking the phone away from my wife was illegal, then why wouldn't the dispatcher have told me that?"

"That's not her job."

"Isn't that entrapment?"

"You're in a very delicate situation here."

"This makes no sense."

"I don't envy you, pal."

"It just seems like I should be able to talk to someone and get this straightened out."

"The domestic violence laws in Connecticut are very stringent these days."

Frenchie launched into a story with roots that were decades old. It was about a Torrington woman named Tracey Thurman who endured years of abuse at the hands of her husband, Charles. One evening, in the summer of 1983, the matter came to a head when Thurman was beaten and then brutally stabbed. During her period of convalescence, and subsequent to her husband's arrest, Thurman filed suit against the Torrington Police Department, claiming they failed to enforce a restraining order. The case marked the first time in the U.S. where a woman sued a town and its police force for a civil rights violation. The lawsuit culminated in Thurman being awarded $2.3 million dollars in damages.

"They even made a movie about it a few years later," Frenchie told me.

"This has nothing to do with me," I maintained. "I'm not abusive. I've never hit my wife. Ever. This is bullshit."

"Connecticut is very strict about domestic abuse."

Officer French and I were having two different conversations. This absurd trend would continue, off and on, for the rest of the time we were together that evening. Despite the momentum of the arrest process, I continued pleading my case, hopeful that compassion would prevail, enlivened by the simple truth that I had done nothing wrong. With unerring focus and self-control, I was able to keep my head together. It would have been too easy to turn unruly and tell "Frenchie" that he was a fascist prick on an obvious power trip and that he could take his domestic abuse laws and shove them up his ass.

Detective M. was not available to talk, so I used the time to call Garr. He didn't answer. I left a message and phoned my father.

"Guess where I am?" I said when he picked up the phone.

My father, whose anxiety level increases even when presented with a rhetorical game, was silent.

"I'm at the Madison Police Station," I said. "They arrested me a little while ago."

Despite whether he hears good or bad news, my father has a habit of immediately relaying the information to my stepmother, who is always at his side.

"Rob was arrested. He's at the station right now."

Then a lot of shock and panic and questions and swearing. Within moments, my father activated his most beloved option on his cordless: speakerphone. Projecting my voice, I relayed a condensed version of what had happened and then listened to them have a two-minute conversation with one another about recourse. Interrupting, I remarked how I was unsuccessful in reaching Garr and would they please make an attempt. As I hung up the phone, the two of them were still going back and forth with one another, debating and conjecturing and disbelieving the entire ordeal.

Next I asked to speak with Phil, DHHS' resource officer. Since my wife had been outed, Phil had been in regular contact with me, checking in during my planning period, offering condolence and

70

unsentimental advice. There was an inane optimism in me that believed Phil could get me off the hook, that his charm and likability could somehow exonerate me. I pictured him bursting through the doors of the booking room, flashing his boyish grin and making some hyperbolic joke that they got the right man, that it was high time they bagged Madison's most lethal miscreant. But I was told that he was on the road, so I could only speak with him by phone.

"You hanging in there, bro?" he asked.

"I'm in shock, Phil. How can this be happening?"

"Just be cool and let it play out."

"I can't believe this. Is there any way…"

How could I even finish the sentence? It was beyond him.

"The laws are strict, bro. It's a real tough situation – for everyone."

His voice, delicate and steady, came through the phone like it was being served on a butler's tray. The poor bastard. I slipped into immediate self-loathing for putting him in the position where he was forced to tell me that there wasn't a thing he could do for me, that I had to let it play out, as he said, that I was alone in this and it was absolutely for real. The talk ended with Phil telling me to call him if I needed anything and that he would check in with me on Monday. When I hung up the phone, I took up a new cause.

"Any chance in keeping this out of the newspapers?"

Frenchie looked at me like I had insulted him in a foreign language.

"That's going to be tough," he said, walking me towards the holding cell.

"But can't you control that? Can't you talk to someone about keeping it from the media?"

Frenchie took a deep breath as he unlocked the heavy metal door and flung it open.

"We don't really have a say in that matter. The media does its own thing."

What could I say? My words had failed me, proving either self-sabotaging or useless. All I could do was shake my head and walk inside the steel cage. Frenchie told me he'd be back in a bit, that he had to process my paperwork. I ended up sitting on a cold metal bench for the next twenty minutes, forcing myself to think of nothing, mired in the fluorescent haze and antiseptic stink of a place I knew had housed vagrants, drunks, and domestic abusers through the years.

When Frenchie reappeared with my paperwork, he told me I had a scheduled court date in 48 hours. Then he asked if there was anyone I might trouble to pick me up. I shook my head. My parents and my sister were an hour away. The thought of waiting it out for them to arrive actually made me shiver. And there wasn't a single friend I was about to burden with such a degrading task.

"Let's go," he finally said.

My options, like my spirits, had been severely compromised. So I climbed into the backseat of Frenchie's cruiser and he drove me to my house. Once there, I was escorted upstairs and monitored as I filled a small overnight bag with clothes, my tablet, magazines, and toiletries. My wife and mother-in-law waited with Robbie and Riley in the kitchen.

"Can I say goodbye to my kids?" I asked Frenchie.

"Of course," he said. "But quickly."

I kept it together long enough to hug and kiss them both and tell them I would see them soon. Then I got in my car and sped through the darkness to my mother's house, an hour north of Madison. It was January 31st, and the menacing reality of how this would be the longest and worst year of my life forced my attention on my big mouth and the trouble it had caused. My mouth needed an intervention, I thought. And fast.

Dear Mouth,

What the fuck? Do you have any self-control? Please don't answer that. In fact, don't even respond to this letter. Just ruminate over what it says. Sure, you and I have had some good times together through the years. Remember Mr. White's History class back in high school? Pretty hilarious. We entertained for hours, turning sophomoric humor into an art form - or at least trying to. Some thought it was a worthy investment of their time. Others did not. But we ignored the latter, didn't we? And remember that wonderful diatribe we unleashed freshman year of college when Pete and Jeremy brought a case of beer to my dorm room the very first week of classes? That R.A. had no idea what hit her.

It goes back even further, doesn't it? Middle school might be where it really began. Probably to Mrs. C.'s class. I recall that morning when I was caught chewing gum, which was unmitigated contraband in her eyes. She sermonized the class on what she called a "vile habit" before exiting the room for a moment. I barely hesitated before rising and extemporizing on the matter: "Our rights are being tampered with. We must stand united in this cause. Mrs. C. is the only teacher who does not allow gum in her class and it's time we did something about it. We have the right to exercise our jaws. We have the right to blow bubbles. And by God, we have the right to smell like watermelon at any hour of the day!" Turned out she was within earshot in the hall and would rain hell on me. Ah, the endless memories.

Mouth, we've made a good team you and I, amusing and shocking friends and strangers alike. We've even fooled some into thinking we're smarter than we actually are. I suppose when you always have something to say, and when you say it with a tinge of self-effacement, it may be confused as intelligent rhetoric. This is not say that our purpose has merely been self-serving. On the contrary. You have shown an unwavering allegiance in the fight against stupidity and thoughtlessness and unfairness.

There was that Stop & Shop rent–a–cop who scared the hell out of Robbie when I failed to spot some groceries he was sitting on. There was that morning at Daniel Hand High School when I was berated in the hall by my former boss, B.B., just as students were passing, and you waited until the end of the day to request a more opportune time for admonishment. And who could forget that cop, Officer Petersen, who went berserk when I ran a red light while taking the kids to the doctor in Essex. You pulled off one hell of a feat that day, my friend, keeping your vitriol just out of earshot of Robbie and Riley, who sat dutifully in the back seat, waiting to see how Daddy would react to this rude prick.

I know you have fantasies about rising to incendiary levels of poetic rambling like Al Pacino in the final scene of Scent of a Woman. Doesn't everyone want to "take a flamethrower" to some institution or another? You and I are hardly unique in that respect. We are, however, unique in that we never censor ourselves. There's a limit. You've got to discriminate. Yes, you've often come through for me; no doubt there. You've helped me land a few jobs over the years and score a few gigs for the band. You've been a particular asset when it's come to girls, assailing them with torrents of inane bullshit that have quite literally amused their pants off. But for every charmed ingénue, there's been a pissed off professor or boss or grocery store security guard or traffic cop who have furrowed their brow and thought, or said, "What a little pissant." They have then exacted a punishment that is as much a personal revenge ploy as it is legal or ethical justice.

Let's face it, Mouth, we're getting older. Don't get me wrong, you haven't lost a step. If anything, you've gotten sharper and quicker and just plain better. The truth is, I'm proud of you, you sly bastard. It's because of you that I've been able to walk through this life as though I'm 6'2" when I'm clearly not. But to be honest, you've become a liability. You hardly ever dial it down. Again, we're getting older. And with age comes grace and restraint. I know you know this. We've certainly gone over it time and time again through the years. It seems as though we feel that this acknowledgement alone is an adequate destination. So we slip back into that old familiar way of ready, aim, fire. Not sure we can afford to do this any longer. I know I'm a buzzkill. But think about it this way: It's pretty difficult to walk around like we're 6'2" after you've gotten my name and picture in the fucking newspaper. I'm not saying it's over between us – God knows we'll still have fun on occasion – but we need to pull back a little, act our age, tame the beast, whatever. It breaks my heart, but it's for the best. Let's leave it at this: We'll see what happens.

Yours truly,
Rob

Chapter 4

As I made the drive to my mother's house, I couldn't help but think that I should have taken Robbie and Riley with me. How could I not have? Would the cops have objected? Was it even an option? All that had happened in the last few hours – the 911 call, the police invasion, the mugshots, the fingerprints – had clouded my thinking. It seemed that I was entering into some brand new state of mind that was trying to tell me I was an actual criminal; I therefore needed to behave accordingly. The desperate, solitary move to my mother's house thus seemed appropriate. As did the phone call I made to my boss, informing him of my arrest.

"I'm sorry to be calling you on a weekend," I said.

"Never a problem," T.J. said.

He meant it, too. T.J. had given me his cell number a few weeks earlier and asked that I call if I needed anything. This marked the first time I used it.

"There was an incident tonight."

He listened intently as I relayed to him the details of the evening. When I finished, he managed to say the one thing I was hoping he would:

"I can't believe they arrested you."

"Jesus Christ, I'm sorry, T.J. I'm sorry you have to deal with this. I don't know what else to say."

"You don't need to apologize."

"I do. I absolutely do."

"Just get to where you're going and I'll be in touch."

I thanked him before apologizing some more. He took a deep breath and paused for a moment before saying what must have been on his mind since January 7th:

"I honestly think people are just going to be shocked that you didn't kill her."

When I hung up the phone, I cursed myself for forgetting to bring up a rather pressing concern: the safety of my job.

"You can have the upstairs all to yourself," my mother told me when I arrived. "I just finished making up the bed for you."

The second floor runs the length of the house and is broken up into a bedroom, bathroom, living room, and office area. Often a source of intrigue as well as hide-and-go-seek for Robbie and Riley, it's entirely unused space by my mother and stepfather. I threw my one bag on the bed and sat in a chair in the dark for a few moments. There were faint traces in the air of old cigarette smoke that had risen from the ground floor from when my mother would default to her bad habit behind her husband's back. It reminded me of my childhood. Back then, it was overt, in plain sight of her first husband, my father, whose disdain for unhealthy living has always been as much of a distinguishing characteristic as his curly hair or broad shoulders.

As I sat there in the dark, I began thinking of my childhood home, a big four bedroom green and brick Colonial on a cul-de-sac in a dream neighborhood. It was something I once obsessed over, prior to having my own family. Secretly, I envied my friends whose parents had remained together and still lived in the same house for decades. What a privilege it would be, I thought, to show off where Daddy once slept and played and got into trouble. As time went on, and I planted my own roots, this became less of a concern.

Absorbed in the moment, and mired in feeling like a little boy once again, and in the worst possible way, I was summoned to dinner by my mother who was calling my name from the bottom of the stairs. Without answering, I forced myself up and made my way to the kitchen.

"I made your favorite," she said, pushing a plate of spaghetti and meatballs in front of me.

It must have killed her that comfort food was about the closest I was going to come to a reprieve. Mopey as a fragile teenager, I sat slumped in my chair, taking tiny, intermittent bites. Rich, my stepfather, didn't miss a beat when he poured me a tall glass of his favorite Cavit white wine.

"Drink up," he said, raising his own glass to me, but not actually making a toast. "We've got well over a case of this stuff."

Rich, then approaching two decades as my mother's husband, looks every bit the former athlete that he is. Standing at 6'2", with hands like road signs, he could have easily chosen his lot in life as a bully. Such a pastime turns out to be the antithesis of who he is. With a full head of thick, gray hair, and gentle, hazel colored eyes, Rich not only makes friends wherever he goes, but he truly sees the good in all people. For a cynic, it can be a frustrating proposition made even more so when you learn just how sincere he is. From the day I met him, I was happy my mother would be his wife. By having the good sense to mock the enterprise of stepfatherhood – he calls himself my Evil Stepfather – he denounced the notion that a power struggle might ever ensue between us. Truth be told, Rich appears to be a far better match for my mother than my own father.

After downing the wine, I asked for a second glass. My mother encouraged me to not drink alcohol on an empty stomach. So I forced an appetite and began to eat. The three of us sat there, under the vilest of circumstances, eating and drinking, them expressing disgust for my wife, and me shaking my head, mumbling how I still couldn't believe I had just been arrested.

"Fucking Madison Police Department," I said. "After I cooperated with them."

We all knew I was referring to the tape I made and handed over just weeks earlier.

"It shows such a lack of compassion," my mother said, fighting back tears.

"What did they say before they arrested you?" Rich asked, putting a few more bottles of wine in the fridge.

I started from the beginning, when my wife and mother-in-law took my children out for the day, and ended with me getting in my car and driving to Vernon. I knew it was a story my muscle memory would soon master and file away in my brain under the category of *permanent infamy.*

Dinner lasted a long time. I discovered, probably through the many refills of white wine, that I could not turn off my brain. My mother and Rich, offering kind words as well as any wisdom they could muster, were willing to listen. After killing three bottles of the Cavit, it was around 11:00. Thanking them for all they had done for me, I announced that I was heading upstairs for the night.

Shutting off my thoughts was impossible. They were circling my head like reels of disjointed movie footage. With no linear sense to any of them, they taunted me in their incompleteness. How would things play out? My kids. My job. My arrest. My court appearance on Monday. Sitting in the dark at the foot of the bed, I felt myself sobering up. With this came a complete thought. Finally. It was a bittersweet revelation: Never again would I live under the same roof as Allison. For three full weeks, since her double life had been exposed, we had been forced to share our home together. This was the most surreal time I had spent in my life. It was all anguish with no catharsis. Black comedy with no punchline. It was days and nights filled with sad and sometimes hostile conversations that amounted to little more than examining the severity of what she had done. It was exhausting. Living with my mother and Rich, until I figured out what would become of me, would be a much needed break.

For the next half hour, I flipped mindlessly through a few Guitar World magazines I had brought with me. Then I tried watching TV. Focusing proved impossible. I knew sleeping would be as well. It was after midnight and I wanted to rest, to turn off my brain. So I went to the top of the staircase and listened for noises below. The quiet told me my mother and Rich had gone to bed. With the lights off, I descended the stairs and tiptoed in the dark towards the kitchen. I somehow managed to find the fridge without walking into a wall. When I opened it, the kitchen instantly fell under a shadowy light that made it seem as though I had created the room right then and there. The door was lined with several bottles of the Cavit. I swiped one that was a little more than half full and forced myself to chug it on the spot. Then I headed back upstairs, my entire body writhing from the sudden intake of so much alcohol, and waited to pass out in the bed my mother had made up for me.

.   .   .   .   .

I woke the following morning to a violent headache and some serious dry-mouth – not to mention an epic snowfall that had begun at around 4:00 a.m. I turned on my cell phone and put it on the nightstand next to me. Then I opened Netflix on the tiny 8" tablet I had thrown in my overnight bag and started watching *Californication*, which contained enough hedonism and nudity to distract me for reasonable bursts of time. Staying under the covers well into late afternoon, I gave new meaning to binge watching as I began to resemble some bedridden catatonic. My mother checked on me a few times, no doubt to see that I hadn't offed myself. My sister and her family braved the weather to come see me. I barely talked. And I ate next to nothing of the breakfast and lunch that were served to me in bed. Too spent to be at all self-conscious over how I pathetic I appeared, I just laid there, balancing the tablet against the pillow on my stomach, watching David Duchovny's character bang everything in sight either before or after bouts of nihilistic self-loathing. On occasion, I would make my way to the window to view the accumulating snowfall and wonder about my court appearance the following day.

Early that evening, I received an unlikely phone call. It was from Officer French. He wanted to see how I was holding up. If I wasn't so depressed, I might have assumed a different voice and a false identity – my non-existent brother, perhaps – before revealing to him that Rob Marchese had just taken his own life. The devastation of the arrest, I would have said, did poor ol' Rob in. His wife's indiscretions combined with the humiliation from the previous night was too much, so he got his hands on a large caliber pistol and fired a bullet into his mouth early this morning. A note was left, I would say, acknowledging that there were no hard feelings towards Officer French and how he was merely doing his job and that no one should place blame or judgment on this dutiful public servant. This would have no doubt made the renegade asshole shit himself in silence. After a few moments, I would have broken character, reclaimed myself, and announced the tasteless joke.

What happened instead was I listened to Officer French, who seemed to be fulfilling some perfunctory order by making the call, ask if I felt emotionally stable, if I had a place to stay, blah, blah, blah. Questions he likely could have asked the previous night.

"I'll be fine," I said. "Thanks for the call."

"One more thing. About your arrest – my supervisor said we can possibly keep it from the media. No promises, but we'll try."

This was something. I surmised that Detective M. was behind it. A small consolation. Perhaps his way of acknowledging how shitty it was that the Madison Police accepted my help a few weeks earlier before they decided to act out their badass cop fantasies on me for emptying a pocketbook. I took it in stride as I thanked Officer French again before hanging up. A second phone call I would receive within the following hour would bring with it some *actual* good news.

"I spoke with the boss," T.J. said, referring to Tom, Madison's superintendent, "and you have nothing to worry about where we're concerned."

"My job is secure?"

"He indicated to me that it's not at all in jeopardy. The three of us will need to meet, but it won't be for an exit interview."

"That's a relief."

"I'm sorry you're going through this."

"The arresting officer just called me. They're going to try and keep it out of the papers."

"I heard."

He didn't need to say more. It dawned on me that it wasn't Detective M. or the tape I had given to him. It was T.J. and Tom who were behind this. It would have been nice to have thought that the gesture was purely magnanimous, but I knew it was steeped more in protecting the reputation of the district. I was fine with this.

"What now?" I asked.

"Just stay out of trouble."

I assured him I would. It killed me to tell him I wouldn't make it to work on Monday since I'd be in court.

"Assuming it's not snowed out," I said.

"I'd plan on going if I were you."

I thanked him for the news. Then I hung up and headed downstairs to see my family and reveal to them that I still had a job. Rich poured me a drink. This time, we toasted our glasses.

•   •   •   •   •

By morning, towns throughout Connecticut were covered with an average of 12-15 inches of snow. Driving conditions were described as "treacherous." The lack of a travel ban left weatherman and commuters bewildered. There were countless spinouts and accidents, and pervasive news footage to prove it. Schools all over the state – including those in Madison – were delayed or cancelled altogether. Even my lawyer opted to stay off the interstate and not risk an accident.

"You'll be fine," Garr told me when I spoke to him that morning. "There's no reason for me to go. They'll make a decision as to whether or not you'll be allowed to return home. Call me this afternoon and let me know what happened."

Before hanging up, he gave me some good news: Through Allison's attorney, he heard that she had given consent for me to move back into the house. I was conflicted. I was desperate to be back home with Robbie and Riley, yet the thought of living once again with their mother was macabre.

"Strange," I said.

"Let me know how things play out."

"Any advice for today?"

"Be cordial and honest."

"Any predictions?"

"None."

"None?"

"Call me later."

"Rich is going with you," my mother told me over a quick

breakfast.

I wanted to refuse the offer. Go alone. Face the weather and the judge and the unknown all by myself. I might have been badly broken, but I could still muster some dignity when necessary. But this, I suppose, was hardly the time for pride.

"I can't believe I have to go," I said, folding the paperwork Officer French had given to me and stuffing it in my back pocket.

"Well, you do," my mother told me.

"Ridiculous. They arrest me on bullshit charges and then make me drive through a blizzard to discuss it."

"You have no choice."

"Looks that way."

She implored me to not be a wiseass in court. Her nerves were on edge that Garr was not going with me. Show humility, she said. Be soft-spoken. Deferential. I looked at Rich, who was nodding in agreement. They were both learning a side of me that was not particularly attractive.

I maintained an average speed of 30mph on the way to the courthouse. Snow was still falling. Few vehicles were on the interstate. Rich, probably in an effort to take my mind off the drive, told me about his marriage and divorce and how it affected his children. He told me how this thing that was happening to me was devastating my mother.

"She cries a lot," he said.

Not what I wanted to hear. I had little to say about this. Turning on the car stereo, I asked Rich if he minded a little music. He shrugged. What I ended up playing couldn't have been more fitting for the moment. "Isn't it a Pity" by George Harrison. The title alone seemed a flawless epitaph to a tragedy still in its nascent stages. The same could be said of the song's opening lines: "Isn't it a pity / Now isn't it a shame / How we break each other's hearts / And cause each other pain." More poignant is Harrison's first guitar break that starts 2:19 into the tune. At barely twenty seconds, it has within it enough sorrow to bring about an almost panic-stricken depression. I've always loved it. But at that moment it had an entirely new resonance to it. It sounded dirge-like. True grownup sadness. By the time the next verse started, I shut it off. It was all too much. The blizzard. The drive. The music. The occasion.

We managed to make it to 235 Church Street in one piece. There was the parking. Then the metal detectors. Then the bailiff with a big belly and receding hairline who told us where to take a seat in the first floor lobby. He would investigate who I needed to see. Rich and I sat there and looked around at the cavernous foyer decked out in cold, drab white marble from floor to ceiling. The place was unrelenting in its bleakness. As we waited, barely talking, we watched people scurry around with a sense of urgency. Their footsteps echoed with mock importance, inviting people watchers to kill time by playing a guessing game. Were these criminals? Stenographers? Judges? Lawyers? Laypersons? It hardly mattered. They all wore the same solemn expression. It was as though any joy they could have had with them might have tripped the metal detectors at the front entrance. With George Harrison's plaintive song still sounding in my head, I began to scrawl some lyrics on the back of the paperwork I had brought with me. By the time I was told where to report – third floor, Room F – a half hour had passed and I had finished the song, which I had begun days earlier. Everything about it was simple. Its title and cadence and rhyme scheme. Even the chords I had in mind.

"Damage Done"

Dreams fall from my head as I sleep
Tears fall from my eyes as I weep
Over damage done (x4)
I promised to write a song for you
Maybe a murder ballad or two
Over damage done (x4)
You're useless as the stars at night
You're trying like hell to shine your light
Over damage done (x4)
The levee's gone and the river is dry
A hard rain's falling from the sky
Over damage done (x4)

The damage done
The air I breathe
They both bring me to my knees...to my knees
The damage done
Is in my home
It's in my blood and in my bones...it's in my bones

I lost my cards and I lost my hand
I lost my brothers and I lost my band
Over damage done (x4)
It's time to celebrate my ghost, so raise your glass and make a toast
Over damage done (x4)
Say a prayer and make it fast...and make your peace with the past
And the damage done (X4)
Sing farewell one time, my dear
Sing it strong and sing it clear
Over damage done (x4)

The damage done, the air I breathe
They both bring me to my knees...to my knees
The damage done is in my home
It's in my blood and in my bones...it's in my bones

A tall woman with brown shoulder length hair introduced herself to me as D.K., Family Relations Counselor. She neither smiled nor shook my hand. Rich and I exchanged a quick glance.

"Follow me," she said.

Rich, who was asked to sit tight outside courtroom F on one of the wooden benches, waited for her to be out of earshot before calling after me:

"Be good. Stay calm."

D.K. led me to her office, which was divided into a handful of empty cubicles. We sat in silence for a few moments while she poked around on her computer. When she pulled up whatever documents she was searching for, she informed me that a decision would be rendered this morning as to whether I would be allowed to move back into my house. Then she asked me to tell her about my familial issues.

"How far back would you like me to go?"

"As far back as you'd like."

I reminded her of the obvious, that I was without my attorney, and therefore wasn't certain what was expected of me.

"Why don't you just tell me what happened - what got you arrested."

This required pretext. So I started as far back as January 7th when I found out about my wife's double affair with underage boys. I talked about her dismissal from Daniel Hand High School. The pending criminal investigation against her. The stress of living together under such impossible circumstances. The state of my marriage and family. And, finally, my arrest on January 31st, just two days ago, for emptying a pocketbook.

Keeping it mostly to the facts, I was calm and soft-spoken, so much so that I began to grow self-conscious of my own voice. D.K. asked a few follow-up questions - mostly about the history of my marriage - and took some notes on her computer. She asked to see the paperwork given to me by the Madison Police Department.

"Sort of an arrest *receipt*, isn't it?" I said, handing it over to her.

She didn't smile. Her approach was businesslike. Nothing more. I imagined she had been on the job for twenty plus years, and in that time had heard some horror stories. Drugs. Neglect. Violence. Abuse. To move her emotionally, I would have had to pluck my bloody, beating heart from my chest cavity and drop it on her keyboard.

"Is that your father you came with this morning?"

"He's my stepfather."

"Why don't you go wait with your stepfather and I'll be with you shortly," she said, handing the papers back to me.

Rich and I sat together on the bench outside of courtroom F for a few minutes before D.K returned and asked to speak with me in private. I followed her a few paces towards a balcony that overlooked the floor below. I remember thinking what a bad idea it was to have a perfect human launching pad in a place with constant acrimony.

"I've spoken with the judge and we feel it would be unwise for you to move back into your house at this time. We will be issuing a protective order against you, which I will explain in a moment. You will therefore need to find a place to reside while this matter is being handled."

Taking a deep breath, I peeked over the edge of the balcony at the shuffling people below. I was clueless to their misery. And they to mine.

"This is unbelievable. I didn't do anything but empty a pocketbook."

"Be that as it may…"

"Not to mention, if I understand correctly, my wife has given her consent for me to move back home. Into *my* house."

"We understand that, but…"

"This proves that she does not feel at all threatened by me. Wouldn't you agree?"

"Mr. Marchese…"

"If she felt threatened, she would not have given her consent."

"Mr. Marchese."

"Not that I *want* to live with her, but I have every right to live in *my* house with *my* children."

"Mr. Marchese."

"I'd like to speak with the judge."

"Mr. Marchese."

"I'd like to speak with the judge."

She took a deep breath. At that moment, I must have suddenly appeared more like her typical clientele.

"I'd like to speak with the judge," I said again.

I said this over and over, not knowing if it was even an option. My desperation, though contained, was fully formed. She stared at me for a moment before asking that I once again sit and wait. After another few minutes, I was brought inside empty courtroom F where I would be given the opportunity to plead my case. In no way did I feel ill equipped to do this. Foolishly, I believed that it was a matter of common sense and human decency. The facts, I reasoned, were incontrovertible: I have no history of violent acts; I did nothing egregious to get arrested; I need to be with *my* children in *my* home; Allison is the one who committed true criminal acts.

D.K. told me to approach the bench and wait for the judge. Rich, who was allowed to be present, seated himself in the rear of the courtroom. A bailiff entered through a corner door adjacent to the judge's chambers. Soon, a court reporter appeared. Then, after five minutes or so, the judge. A female judge. Probably in her early forties, with boyishly short brown hair and a round, pleasant face, she looked more like a camp director than someone who decides the fate of those who stand before her. Introductions were made, formalities recited, and I was given the opportunity to speak. With the humblest demeanor I could muster, I went over my ordeal once again. I spoke evenly, making seamless eye contact and pausing from time to time to catch my breath and offer the kind of smile that has within it a quiet sense of pleading.

"May I see the paperwork you've brought with you today," the judge asked.

I handed it over and watched her read it. My eyes were fixated on the lyrics I had written on the back. I half hoped she might turn the paper over and read my pathetic song. This might have given the matter a new emotional angle. She didn't. Instead, she asked me to continue speaking, which I did. When I was finished, the judge looked over some additional documents and asked me questions about where I lived and worked. I tried to make my answers as long as possible, either to show I was confident and of sound mind, or to stave off the bad news I knew was inevitable.

"I cannot grant you permission to move back into your house."

It took a lot to hold back the smug "Well then fuck you" grin I felt creeping across my face.

"I don't understand."

"The court is not at all comfortable allowing such a move to take place. Your situation appears to be quite volatile."

It would have been nearly comical to argue this point. The decision had been made. Again. I exhaled a little, slouched my posture, and listened to her run down a list of concerns about the potential for more domestic violence. She used this phrase over and over – "domestic violence" – which instantly played like some foreign mantra that figured not at all in my life. Even as my spirit was being eviscerated, I had instant fantasies about turning myself into a martyr and railing against the system. Bombastic yet eloquent voice. Lyrical yet accessible language. I wanted to cite legal precedents and actual cases and silence the judge into submission. I wanted to make the court reporter type furiously and the bailiff fumble for his phone so he could record my glorious onslaught. I wanted to make Rich a little nervous before he'd give himself over to his stepson's brilliantly sensible rant.

Instead, I was explained the conditions of the protective order: *The defendant is not to threaten, assault, stalk, or harass the victim in any way. The defendant is not to visit or enter the residence of the victim except for a scheduled visit, accompanied with the police, to retrieve some personal effects. The defendant is not to text or phone the victim.*

"Do you understand these conditions we've just gone over?"

I nodded my head.

"I need a verbal response."

"Yes. I do."

Looking at a calendar, the judge then scheduled a future court date to review the matter further; then she told me to have a nice day before releasing me back into the wild winter snowstorm.

•   •   •   •   •

"That's what I expected," Garr said when I spoke to him that evening. "We'll just have to go back to court and make a motion to get you back into the house."

"Are you coming with me next time?"

"I plan to."

"You *plan* to?"

"My presence today wouldn't have changed this outcome."

"How do you know that?"

"Trust me."

If this guy was a surgeon, I thought, his patients would perform their own operations.

"You can stay here as long as you need to," my mother told me over dinner. "Don't think twice about it. We've got the room and we love having you."

I was appreciative, yet the hour long commute to work would be brutal – especially given recent weather trends. But the more pressing matter was my kids. I felt physically ill over the separation. The day had enervated me to the point where I didn't even feel like complaining. I took a bottle of wine upstairs and commenced to binge watching *Californication*. After a few glasses and two or three episodes of the show, my mother paid me a visit.

"I've been checking the news all day," she said, "and there's been no report of your arrest."

I nodded.

"So that's good."

"I guess."

"Do you need anything?"

"Revenge."

"Do you need anything else? Something a mother can offer her son."

I was silenced by her kindness. Sweet offer, but nothing more than a perfunctory gesture. I needed my children, my dignity, my home. We sat there for a while, just the two of us, saying nothing, listening to our breathing and the sound of the basketball game Rich was watching in the living room below us. She gave no advice or words of wisdom. I remember thinking how she lost her parents very early on in her adulthood. Twenty-seven when her mother died. Thirty-one for her father. Both to cancer. This was something she almost never talked about. Not when I was little and could have cemented some mythologized image of them in my mind. And not when I was older and could have appreciated them as real living and breathing people who happened to be my grandparents. She must have been wrecked by their premature passing. Decades of *nothing* when there could have been something. Dinners. Phone calls. Visits. Vacations.

My mother's presence in my life thus became a silent triumph. I was glad as hell she was alive. I needed her to see me through this. Yet, like the passing of her own parents, my ordeal would change who she had become.

"This is all I need for now," I said, answering her earlier question by pouring another glass of wine.

That night I fell into a deep sleep and had dreams of chord progressions for my new song. My beleaguered brain must have known two things: 1) That I was excited to have lyrics for a new tune – especially one that came about so quickly, and 2) That words on a page, words that were bleak and visceral, words written while sitting on a New Haven courthouse bench awaiting bad news, were about all I had going for me.

Dear Mom,

You're forgiven for not attending my martial arts tournaments and football games. Especially the football games. If you recall, my team was pretty awful. One winning season in four years. We went 7-3. I was a senior. That was pretty sweet. Martial arts, though, is a somewhat different story. I'm not reneging on that forgiveness, mind you. But weren't you at all enticed when I began coming home every month with a new trophy? Dad and I used to go to Maine and New Hampshire and Atlantic City – all over the east coast, really – where we'd hone the bohemian lifestyle together. Hotels. Diners. Late nights. More than anything, though, he and I were bonding. Maybe what we forged together seemed impervious to you – and maybe in a way it was – so you threw up your arms and resigned over the matter. I understand. I'm far from scarred over anything you or Dad did while I was growing up. We had a good run there for a while. Before your divorce. It's not like I need to confide in a therapist because when I was sixteen Mommy didn't watch me battle it out with some nameless opponent in a dank, airless gymnasium in Woonsocket.

It seems we've done our own bonding lately. Just you and me. Not really what either of us had in mind. That's for sure. But bonding is bonding, I suppose. We've starred in our own little movie, haven't we? It's the one where the kid is grown, maybe moderately successful, slightly disenfranchised, yet he reconnects with a parent, always under extreme circumstances, and attempts to address some heretofore unresolved issue. They fight. They share. They relive. They may even change a little. Tom Hanks and Jackie Gleason made a good one back in 1986 with Nothing in Common. Ewan McGregor and Christopher Plummer made one in 2010 with Beginners. There's Everybody's Fine with Robert DeNiro. The Savages with Philip Seymour Hoffman. Affliction. Five Easy Pieces. I could go on. The thread that binds all these films is that the parental figure is the father rather than the mother. So there's some additional incentive for me to actually write this little flick of ours.

I understand you more than I did before. The way you love and fight and protect. I've seen all this firsthand and up close. Closer than I ever did in all my childhood. This stands to reason; the stakes, after all, have been far greater and the emotions more acute. This, I suppose, is what happens when you watch your child's life fall apart.

On another note, I'm sorry for your sadness. Truly. It's a violent storm we got caught in. Your heart breaks for me, and I in turn feel guilty and thus become more dispirited, and you react accordingly, and the cycle goes on. Still, the grace you've shown through this thing has been something worth mentioning. You somehow knew just when to be silent or when to grieve or when to reign me in. Christ, I might have been arrested two or three more times had you not done so.

Maybe there have been private moments you've had when you wished you had died before bearing witness to all that has happened. You don't need to confirm or disconfirm this. I certainly wouldn't blame you one bit. But for my own sake, I'm glad you've been here to see me through it. I detest all things maudlin and I'm trying not to go there. Yet I know how to circumvent this; just throw the word "fuck" somewhere in the sentiment. Observe. The fucking havoc wrought on my life would have been tenfold had it not been for you. The fucking support you've shown has left me awestruck. The fucking debt I owe to you is beyond measure.

Don't I know just how to make a mother proud?

Love,

Rob

Chapter 5

There was no way I could continue living in Vernon. It was fine for a layover while I considered my options, but at an hour away from work and my kids' daycare and school, it was too far. Ejected from my Madison house by the New Haven Superior Court, and with the long winter months looming, my options were sparse. The cost of an academic rental while continuing to pay my mortgage was not doable. Even a cheap motel – such a depressing thought – would be too expensive. Friends and colleagues began to offer me their sofas or spare rooms. One even had a finished basement he said was mine for the taking. All lovely offers, but the imposition would be too great. With a shared custody agreement, I needed a place I could bring my children and be comfortable. As grateful as I was over the generosity of these people, I couldn't imagine huddling in a bedroom with Robbie and Riley, constantly shushing them out of deference to our host. Allison, meanwhile, continued to live in our home. Jobless and awaiting her fate, she subsisted on her pay, which she would continue to receive for the next several months.

My attorney filed a motion for her to vacate the home, but she had the luxury of time on her side. She first had to find a place to live. This was not going to be easy. With her February 11th arrest, her case had escalated overnight, receiving widespread publicity. I learned that news crews had camped out on my front lawn and that Allison was receiving propositions from men as far away as Saudi Arabia.

"I need to get my kids away from her," I told Garr. "And I need to get back inside my house."

"One thing at a time."

After another week of living with my mother and stepfather, an offer fell into my lap. John, a friend and colleague, approached me in my classroom one morning with the gift of an in-law apartment.

"We're not renting it out," he said. "It's just sitting there. Heather and I discussed it and you can stay as long as you want."

Having been to John's house in Old Saybrook, I had seen the place he was talking about. It was perfect.

"Think about it," he said.

He added that this was a free offer.

"That's insane," I said. "I'm not sure what to say."

He smiled boyishly. Tall and thin and sporting scholarly glasses, John always reminded me of one of those all-American WWII-era soldiers you see photos of in documentaries – the earnest looking kind who isn't thrilled about heading off for battle, but knows he's making his parents and community proud. Over the years we drank a few beers together and quoted *The Big Lebowski* a thousand or so times and bonded over our mutual love of *The Joshua Tree* and *Sticky Fingers*. A musician himself, he even sat in with my band when our own drummer had to cancel. Most importantly, he was heartbroken over what had happened to my family and this gesture was his way of saying so.

The in-law apartment turned out to be a wonderful refuge. With its own entrance and parking, the place had a kitchenette, a small bedroom, a living room, and a bathroom with laundry facilities. Robbie and Riley saw it as an adventure; they loved everything about it from the drum kit in the foyer to John's impressive record collection that spanned nearly ten feet of shelf space. Perhaps what they loved the most is that John and Heather's own two children, a little boy and girl, were just next door.

The joy that once accompanied so much in my life – music, time with friends, my children – was now emaciated. I found that all I wanted to do was take sleeping pills and sleep and sleepwalk and dream of sleep and be a case study for researchers who research sleep. Playing music was awkward. Listening to it was painful. Food was a hassle. I lost ten pounds over what seemed like a few days. And there was Robbie and Riley. What could I give them? What could I say to them? I honestly wanted to ship them off to my sister's, crawl into bed, and switch everything to the *off* position. It was impossible to be around them. It was deadly not to be.

Around this time, salon owner Emily and I had begun seeing one another regularly; I was somehow able to get my shit together enough to not scare her away. The comfort of a beautiful girl, as shallow as I knew this was, was sacred enough for me to pretend I was healthy and ready for some kind of relationship. One evening we were at her place, which was mere miles from my own house in Madison. Every so often I would look out the window onto the snow covered front street that ran by her apartment and consider how it led to where I truly wanted to be.

Our date had been pleasant – Chinese food and *Boogie Nights* – and we were now lying in her bed watching the recent snowfall. It was approaching 1:00 a.m. and I was hoping she was going to suggest I spend the night. Instead, she looked at me and asked if I wanted to see her gun.

"You have a gun?"

"I do."

"For real?"

"For real. Do you want to see it?"

"Absolutely."

She walked over to a bureau at the other end of the room and removed a small caliber revolver she brought back into bed with her.

"It's not loaded," she said.

"Why do you have it?"

She explained – a young, single woman living alone. Besides, she told me, she once had a stalker.

"Impressive," I said.

Emily laughed. Then we laid back on her bed and listened to some music on her iPad. Even with the nasty weather, I could have run to my house and up to Robbie and Riley's bedroom in close to twenty minutes. But a protective order said I couldn't. So instead, I holed up with a beautiful girl in her apartment, looking between the accumulating snowfall through her window and the revolver resting on my chest. She never did ask me to spend the night.

It was during my pre-scandal life when I booked R.J. Julia's. At just two miles from my house, R.J.'s was to be the first stop on my book tour to promote *Nine Lies*, my first published novel. My original vision for the event's turnout was modest: colleagues and friends and local bookworms all crammed together in the store, listening to a few excerpts, asking questions about narrative technique, offering congratulations on the book's publication. Of course there would be my wife and two children. They would be front and center. Allison would be watching intently, knowing that the moment was a dream come to life for her husband. My children would see their father vacillate between modesty and bravado. They would understand hardly a word of what was read or spoken; they wouldn't need to. All they would know, based on my tone and expression, not to mention the reception of the crowd, is that I was exactly where I wanted to be.

The reading was scheduled for Thursday, February 19th at 7:00 p.m. I emailed the event coordinator a few days prior to see if she still wanted me. The name "Marchese" was no doubt familiar to her at this point. She replied that they had already ordered copies of the book and that it was expected that people would show. When I arrived at 6:15, I was greeted by an attractive young woman who escorted me to a rear room on the upper level of the store. A round table was piled with tidy stacks of my novel behind a few that were standing up. I took a seat about twenty feet from a few dozen folding chairs.

"Can I get you anything?" she asked.

"Maybe some water."

"One water coming up."

When she smiled at me, my gut ached. I suddenly thought of Emily who hinted to me earlier in the day that she would try to make it. I waited for her to show. I waited for my water. I waited for recognizable faces. I got two out of three. Several of my students showed up. A girl named Tori and a boy named Connor and another boy named Austin, who came with his mother, which made me nearly cry. My favorite work-mommy, Elaine, showed up, dragging with her Russ, her soft-spoken husband. Paul showed up. And Kristin. And a few others. But not Allison. Naturally. And not Robbie and Riley; they were with their mother that evening. Two miles up the street. Probably having dessert or getting into the tub or watching TV.

"Thank you for coming out tonight," I began. "I appreciate the support. I imagine some of you came because you're interested in my book, while others might have come for different reasons altogether. I just want you to know that I accept both camps with open arms."

Some mild laughter. I took a deep breath and began to read the first of the three excerpts I had selected earlier in the day. I was used to having a lot of eyes on me at once. And I was used to reading aloud to large groups. But this was unlike anything I had grown accustomed to from teaching high school students. This was more like theatre. And as with all theatre, it had an element of soul-baring in it. *Nine Lies* is hardly nonfiction, but it still has within it my own words, my own story. I fought to keep a steady voice. Fought to look up on occasion past the open pages at the cluster of gazing voyeurs. Fought to not drop the book to the floor and declare "Fuck it! Fuck this! What's the fucking point? Where's Emily? Where's Allison? Where are my children? Can someone please explain exactly what the hell has happened?"

After the excerpts, I answered a series of questions. Then I signed books and talked a bit with some of my supporters. The room cleared out and I was left alone with a stack of *Nine Lies* and a hoarse voice. The event coordinator thanked me and told me I could choose one free book from anywhere in the store. She said it was a small token of appreciation.

I chose a posthumous Shel Silverstein collection, *Every Thing On It*. Thumbing through the book in my car, it dawned on me that it would be at least a few more days before I would be able to read it to my children. Driving back to the in-law apartment in Old Saybrook, I recognized that the inauspicious evening behind me could end up being the only promotion I would ever do for my book. It was.

•   •   •   •   •

Attorney Garr called me one afternoon in early March and said he wanted to meet. The call came as a surprise. The truth is that I had grown accustomed to not hearing from him for long stretches at a time.

"What's the agenda?" I asked.

"Your case."

"Can you be more specific?"

"It's going to cost a little more than we planned."

"How much more?"

"A *lot* more," he said. "With your arrest, I'm nearly out of the initial retainer."

Ten-thousand-dollars. Gone. All for emptying a pocketbook and making an off-color comment. I met Garr the following week at a New Haven coffee joint. Without having told him, I brought my mother and sister. The four of us ordered drinks before grabbing a table and getting down to business.

"Lawyers are wordsmiths," Garr began, sipping his coffee. "We are in the business of focusing on language. And the language we use becomes a crucial element in our cases. We find creative ways to phrase things and ultimately achieve getting what we're after."

If he had a point, it was either lost on the three of us, or he was building up to it. My mother, realizing this was costing us a few hundred an hour, wasn't interested in waiting:

"So what are you saying?"

"I'm saying I might be able to get you what you want, but the way we *word* it is going to sound misleading. I'm talking about full custody, which is not easy to get."

I pointed out that full custody is what he nearly guaranteed during our initial consultation.

"That's right," my mother pointed out, "what's changed?"

"What's changed is how we're going to word it," Garr said. "We just won't be calling it *full custody*. It'll be more like full decision making. Schooling, medical care – those sorts of matters."

As important as I knew these were, my more pressing concern was how I wanted to physically live with my children twenty-four hours a day, seven days a week.

"That's going to be difficult," Garr said, sipping his coffee.

"That's not what you discussed a few weeks ago," my mother said again.

"There's also the matter of money," Garr said, ignoring her comment, "how far are you willing to go?"

"I think we understand," my mother said in a way that signified that the meeting was over.

Garr finished his drink and we all walked outside. The afternoon was cold and overcast. One of those mobile laundry service vans was parked in front of the coffee joint unloading stacks of fresh dry cleaning.

"Be in touch," Garr said before shaking our hands and walking down the block towards his BMW.

My mother turned towards me and my sister, her expression doused in the afterglow of disgust.

"That was about one thing and one thing only," she said. "Money. He was feeling us out to see how deep our pockets are. Simple as that."

Garr was fired the following week. A call was then made to the law offices of Ray Hassett who was put on retainer for half of what his predecessor charged. Documents were transferred, updates were given, and we thus entered into phase two of the divorce.

•   •   •   •   •

Most of the memories I have of teaching during this time have been wiped clean. I know I went to work. I know I did my job. I know I never once broke down in front of my students or colleagues and lost my shit and stared off into the distance until someone had to either wait for the moment to pass or else ask if I was still orbiting on planet earth. I did my best to remain invisible. I kept to myself, eating lunch alone in my room, waiting until after school to make photocopies, doing whatever I could to spare people the discomfort of having to see me.

Freak show. Punchline. Cuckold. Reject. Spectacle. Poor, poor pitiful me. I couldn't figure how to carry myself. My former identity seemed like it had vanished, and I was left to assimilate to how I was feeling, which was like one of the tragic characters I taught to my students. I was existing, breathing, moving from here to there, often times with an agenda I would forget within seconds. Soon I began writing reminders for myself. MEETING AT 2:00. GRADE TESTS. EAT LUNCH.

Many of my colleagues, some of whom I consider among my closest friends, made it known that they wanted to help. Mark and Pierre and

Dave R. and Pete and Ron and Martin and George and Scott and Elaine and Chrissy and Pegge and Jessica and Patti and Cynthia and countless others visited my room or stopped me in the hall to extend their support. Some offered food. Some, affection. Some, a shoulder to cry on. Some, just blank and bewildered nods as if to say, "Holy God in heaven." One even offered to pay for a trip to Vegas and a hooker when we arrived.

There was of course another faction: the few who had been friendly with Allison. And it's important to note the line between being *friendly* and being *friends*. Allison, for all her charm and affability, truly did not have any friends at DHHS. This was a common complaint of hers. She often bemoaned her social plight in the U.S., citing how she was the popular one in high school and college and had always made friends so easily; this would often segue into a conversation about how Canadians were kinder and more outgoing than Americans.

This is not to say she was a loner. She was not. Our peers liked and respected her. I'm positive they found her cheerful and professional. There was one woman at DHHS - let's call her Aim, the woman who loves anagrams - who occasionally shared a manicure or cup of coffee outside of school with Allison. The aftermath of every one of these outings had my wife reveal to me her true feelings about Aim, the woman who loves anagrams.

"She's miserable. And so spoiled. All she does is complain. About money and aging and her family and how she's not more of a valued member of the English Department. I can only take her in small doses."

I already knew all of this. Everyone did. Aim, the woman who loves anagrams, was a petulant, middle-aged buzzkill who claimed victimhood at every turn. According to her, she was underappreciated, underpaid, and under more stress than the rest of us. Her open contempt towards younger, prettier faculty was as laughable as it was sad. She once announced to a room full of colleagues that she was convinced we all saw her as a tortured artist. When she left the room, someone asked the group in a hushed tone if Aim had even one artistic inclination - she didn't write, paint, sculpt, or draw. She was as status and money obsessed as anyone I've ever met. One afternoon I found her in the English office, close to tears and huddling over some scrap paper.

"You okay?" I asked.

"No," she shot back.

"What is it?"

She told me the problem was that no matter how she crunched the numbers, it seemed quite difficult for her and her husband to make a combined income of $250,000.

"If it's any consolation," I told her, "I can relate."

Brazen and entitled, she one time held court with the school's administration, assailing them with her contempt for a supposed lack of vision and creativity. Those who witnessed the exchange, myself included, initially thought it was an elaborate ruse they were all in on together. A more telling display occurred one year when Lisa, one of the school's most beloved veteran English teachers, was recognized as educator of the year. Lisa's husband had passed within the last six months, yet her devotion to her students had never waned. The ceremony to honor her was a bittersweet triumph. Stoic as always, Lisa accepted her award with aplomb before making a short speech and exiting the stage. Aim, the woman who loves anagrams, was seated next to me. Like the rest of the crowd, she put her hands together and made a pleasant expression. But in the midst of the cheering, she leaned over to me and said something to which I had zero response:

"Apparently, to get recognized in this district, your spouse has to die prematurely."

Allison's only other peer she occasionally socialized with was a woman a few years our senior. Let's call her Martha, named after Edward Albee's brusque protagonist from *Who's Afraid of Virginia Woolf?* Often the loudest and most opinionated one in the room, Martha had conflict with everyone in her path – students, coworkers, family, doctors, neighbors. The way she told it, these people was either stupid, short-sighted, incompetent, or altogether clueless. As far as I could see, Martha possessed not only zero tact, but zero loyalty as well.

One year, a colleague paid a visit to my classroom, letting me know that Martha, in her most strident of voices, unleashed a tirade to a room full of teachers on how the English department were a bunch of second-rate hacks. She named names and ran down a litany of what she felt were major professional, and in some cases, personal, impediments. Another time, over lunch, she shared a lurid tale about fornicating with an entire hockey team back in her college days. One time she announced she was a shoo-in for Jeopardy, as soon as she auditioned. She claimed to be an artist, a soon-to-be comedienne, and in perhaps one of her more bizarre detours from reality, a commissioned screenwriter, hired by her not-in-the-movie-business father who was paying her a generous stipend to write said script.

In the aftermath of Allison being dismissed from DHHS in the early months of 2015, no one knew what to think of the charges. They knew they were serious, but I'm positive there were more than a few, Martha, and Aim, the woman who loves anagrams, among them, who were giving her the benefit of the doubt. A misunderstanding, perhaps. Or a frame job. Or, quite possibly, that I had driven her to madness and ultimately to commit these crimes. Just the thought of this latter group existing was enough for me to lose my mind. I was tight lipped when people asked me about her. My response was always the same:

"Just know this," I'd say, "regardless of what you hear or think or even whatever happens, Allison will never again set foot in this building."

This was the truth. She had, in fact, been officially banned from ever entering any school in the town of Madison. The implications this would have on Robbie and Riley were glaring. Orientations. Teacher conferences. Plays. Sporting events. Allison would miss them all.

•   •   •   •   •

Ray Hassett, my new attorney, inherited a nightmare. My own arrest not only stalled the divorce proceedings, costing an exorbitant sum of money, but temporarily gave Allison the advantage in nearly every way. Unwittingly, I had helped create the perception that I was unstable, a hothead, and possibly abusive. What helped to allay this were the countless people, whether in person or online, claiming that she was lucky I hadn't murdered her.

"You've got to get yourself into therapy," Ray told me. "It'll help. Not to mention, it'll look good, like you're trying to get a handle on the situation."

Therapy, to me, sounded absurd. A waste of time and money. And for what? To state the obvious: that my family has been destroyed and that I am scared for the sake of my children and sick over not seeing them every day and barely functioning or eating and wanting only to be sedated and subsisting on wine and sleeping pills and living a cheerless existence that I am certain will never cease. At that point, I had only the energy for a recommendation, not an actual appointment. So I asked my friend Kerry, a licensed family therapist, and she got back to me within a few days. She thought Jim H. out of Guilford might be a good fit. I thanked her and tacked Jim H.'s number to my bulletin board. Then I contacted Madison Youth & Family Services and found a therapist for my son. He took to it willingly and even looked forward to going for an hour each week. His cooperation caused me to shake my head; I couldn't help but recognize this as being time he should have spent playing Legos in his room or chasing his sister through the yard. Like the rest of us, he would never get that time back again.

•   •   •   •   •

One early afternoon, on a Saturday in mid-March, my mother and I were having lunch in Middletown. We were discussing the details of a trip I would soon be taking to Nashville. It was a DHHS sponsored trip I would be chaperoning.

"You must be looking forward to getting away," my mother said.

"Are you kidding," I said, "I've been dreaming of nothing but the Grand Ole Opry for weeks now."

I was excited about getting out of Connecticut, about bonding with my students outside the classroom, about the normalcy of it all. My mother and sister planned to take Robbie and Riley during these few days, and we were working out the details when I received a text message from my principal: "Brace yourself – your arrest made the paper." Nodding my head, I responded "Gotcha. Thanks." He asked me to take a few days off and return when the matter blew over. I said I would. Cursing Officer Frenchie, I handed the phone to my mother who was speechless at first before telling me no one would hold it against me, that it was understandable, and to eat the lunch I had barely touched.

I returned to work in the middle of that week. Without a lesson plan or agenda, I relied on the expressions of my students, which were as composed as they were forlorn.

"Want to talk?" I asked my first period class. "You must have questions."

They turned to one another. I shrugged and let them know the offer was for real. Only a few moments went by before the first question:

"How are your kids?"

We were off and running. How was I doing and would I be back the following year and what did I say to piss off the Madison Police to get arrested and did I have supportive parents and siblings and what would happen to Mrs. Marchese and would we divorce and would I write a book about it all? With the exception of admitting that I called Mrs. Marchese "the Blowjob Queen of Madison," I answered all of their questions with as much detail as I could. Time flew by. My other three classes also took me up on the offer to cast academics aside and have a Q&A session.

To this day, those few hours remain the most salient affirmation of why I ever entered into the teaching profession. For all that has been said about teenagers through the years – their moodiness and fickleness – they are a special breed. Being on the cusp of young adulthood, with a clear-eyed view to the eventual shitshow in which they will someday star, they must secretly count their blessings that they are not yet their mother or father.

If I needed proof that grownups did in fact suck, I nearly choked on a dose when I returned to work that week. My lawyer, in preparation for the custody battle that was sure to ensue, asked me to procure letters from anyone who could attest to my abilities as a good father. I asked seven friends, all male colleagues. The response from six of them was immediate and heartfelt: "Whatever you need. No problem. Glad to help."

The seventh one – let's call him Jude – seemed to be taking a long time on his letter. I waited a few days before asking him about it.

"I'm not comfortable doing this," he said.

"You mean helping me?"

"Going against Allison."

I couldn't believe what I was hearing. To sympathize with my ordeal, did he need to see the text transcripts of her grooming a fourteen-year-old boy? I tried to set him straight:

"Just for the record, you don't need to mention *her* at all. It would be about *me*. About my abilities as a father, which you've seen."

Jude wasn't sold. He was going to make me work for the letter. It was a striking moment in that it marked the first time I ever felt the acute sensation of a friendship ending at once. It's been my experience for them to burn out over time.

Walking away, I couldn't help but remember two years earlier when Jude had been diagnosed with cancer. This happened when he and I were becoming friends. His condition drew us closer. In the months he took off of work, I sent him letters to lift his spirits, a book on *Archer*, his favorite show, and even a hat for his loss of hair. Once his illness was bested, he planned his wedding to a fellow DHHS teacher. My invitation seemed the ultimate symbol of our friendship. But, like medals pinned to a hero, or affection felt for a whore, it ended up amounting to nothing. I made due with six letters rather than seven.

•   •   •   •   •

My family funneled their worry in different ways, taking shifts with certain priorities. My sister would implore me to make an appointment with Jim H. She would point out the obvious, which was the size of the burden I was carrying, and tell me I should be going to therapy at least once a week. My father and stepmother were all about me protecting my assets and caring for Robbie and Riley. My mother became obsessed with cases similar to Allison's: CT-based teachers and coaches either accused or convicted of having sexual relations with students. She created spreadsheets that delineated the particulars of the twenty or so cases she had researched – charges, pleas, timelines, outcomes – and became a walking Wikipedia page. No conversation about Allison was complete without a barrage of data that might somehow indicate to me the fate of my children's mother.

Relenting finally on the therapy bit, I called friendly faced Jim H. out of Guilford – I researched him online and liked the look of his round, cheerful face – and made an appointment. Jim's office resembled some bohemian girl's college dorm – mismatched rugs arranged haphazardly, yard sale looking furniture with more nicks and scratches than a second-hand Civic, jarred candles resting atop faded doilies, dried flowers in dusty vases on book shelves stacked with countless volumes on human behavior. Jim looked to be in his late forties. Stocky, clean shaven, and with bulbous facial features, he could have had his likeness on the advertisement for some second-rate fast food chain.

Before taking a seat, Jim asked for my copay of thirty dollars. Having played a show a few nights earlier, I had a hundred-dollar bill in my wallet, which I offered him.

"Can I pay for three sessions up front?" I said.

"Are you kidding?" he asked, taking the bill from my hand. "I've never turned down cash in my life and I'm not going to start now."

Laughing a little, he stuffed the hundred in his shirt pocket and asked me to tell him about myself. Considering the crassness of his money remark, I stalled a little. It took me a few moments to shake it off. But before I began, I sheepishly asked for my change. Jim looked at me like I had just interrupted the reading of a will.

"No problem," he finally said, digging the bills from his wallet and handing them to me.

Psyching myself up, I began with what brought me to him. Then I gave him my backstory – my upbringing, my parents' divorce, adolescence. We talked about my job and my children and my concerns for them.

"You ought to be concerned," he said. "I'm not sure how healthy it will be for them to remain in a school district where their mother is so notorious."

"Well, I'm pretty adamant about remaining in Madison."

"I'm not sure that would be in the best interest for your two children."

Nodding slowly, I let Jim continue. He had a lot to say on the matter. My body language, sulky and serious, did nothing to deter him.

"Just some things to consider," he said once he exhausted the topic.

Maybe I was unaccustomed to the goings-on of an average therapy session, or maybe I was still brooding over his tasteless money remark and barrage of common sense, but I nevertheless found myself shutting down. There wasn't a doubt in my head that my time with Jim would be limited.

One late morning in March, some colleagues began to visit my classroom. With grave expressions and hushed tones, they brought with them something very different from the consolation they had bestowed not so long ago. They brought with them warnings. It seemed there was someone in the building who was in regular contact with Allison. And this someone was being fed nasty information they were freely spreading: I was a wife beater, a savage, a miscreant who had practically lived a double life.

I had so many questions. How could people still be speaking with her? How could she lie about me like that? How could a grownup be so catty as to spread gossip during such a trying time? One question I did *not* have was who the culprit was. It had her fingerprints all over it. I thus braced myself for what I knew would be a heavy discussion before paying a visit to Aim, the woman who loves anagrams.

She was alone in her classroom when I popped my head in and asked if we could speak. She invited me in and we sat down across from one another and got down to it.

"Any idea how much I'm dealing with lately?"

"I'm sure it's a lot."

"This is a pretty unbelievable situation."

"Agreed."

"Which is why I don't need additional stress."

"Fine."

"I need to be able to come to work and have some semblance of peace and normalcy."

"Fine."

"Haven't we known each other for years?" I asked.

"We have."

"And isn't it safe to say you have a solid sense of who I am as a person?"

She shrugged. I repeated the question. She still didn't answer.

"I need to be able to know that we can work together without conflict," I said. "Now and in the future."

Again she shrugged.

"I know you and Allison were friendly, but she's gone," I said. "And she *deserves* to be gone. And she's not returning. Not after what she did."

"What exactly did she do?"

It wasn't clear to me whether Aim was actually in the dark or if she simply wanted to gossip. It didn't matter. I was ready and willing to discuss the matter openly. So I did. I expounded on the details – the Instagram exchanges, the selfies, the stalking, the oral sex, all of it.

Afterwards, neither of us spoke for a bit. Then she said something. It was a line that struck me as the pinnacle of who she truly was. It suggested that she *had* known the story all along, but only wished to discuss it further, and face to face with yours truly.

"Do you have any idea what this thing has done to me and my family?"

I waited for her question to cause an earthquake. I was sure it would. It had to. But nothing happened. No undulating motion or tremors of any kind. I responded with the only words that seemed appropriate:

"That has to be the most narcissistic thing any human has ever said."

That did it. Aim, the woman who loves anagrams, began to cry. She cried, while at the same time denying being a narcissist. I watched her for a moment, with the kind of keen interest one might reserve over the spectacle of one insect mauling another. Her tears were for real. And it was at that moment that I realized just how similar to Allison this woman was – selfish, unstable, delusional. More than any of these, she seemed to me to be dangerous. This didn't stop me from rising from my seat, circling toward her, and throwing my arms around her while telling her everything was going to be all right.

My mind was growing preoccupied with the idea of division and disharmony. Things splitting and separating. Two distinct parts. Zoning out one day, and fueled as much by wanderlust as I was by malaise, I Googled a map of the U.S. Kansas City immediately caught my eye. I was taken in by how it's essentially one city splayed across two states. An idea suddenly came to me to write a song where each city represents one half of a doomed relationship.

"Kansas City"

Tell me where you're going / where you been / where you're from / and how come you're leaving
Meet me on the boulevard / on the street / uptown / 'cause downtown can be deceiving
It's a pity and a shame / It's Kansas City in the rain / It's pouring / It's boring / It's true
Let me say goodbye / one more time / a farewell / is hard to sell / when you're blushing
Guilty pleasures fly / on the ground / in the air / but who cares when you're rushing
It's witty and it's dumb / It's Kansas City in the sun / a bar fight by starlight / It's me and you

Kansas City, Kansas City / You're living side by side / You're a single point of pride
You're a rusted double wide in the rain
Kansas City, Kansas City, you been so discreet / You're damn hard to beat / You're a shitload of heartache and pain

Keep your King of clubs / and Ace of spades / and Queen of hearts / and fresh starts by your door

108

Bring me something good / something strong / and make it sweet / and then I'll sleep on your floor
It's a pity and a shame / It's Kansas City in the rain / It's pouring / It's boring / It's true
Your lies are so clean / so fresh / and brand new / and they're true when you're trying
The past is such a scam / it's over here / it's over there and everywhere and dead and dying
It's witty and it's dumb / It's Kansas City in the sun / a bar fight by starlight / It's me and you

Kansas City, Kansas City / You're living side by side / You're a single point of pride
You're a rusted double wide in the rain
Kansas City, Kansas City, you been so discreet / You're damn hard to beat / You're a shitload of heartache and pain

My exchange with Aim, the woman who loves anagrams, introduced me to another brand new problem: walking the halls of DHHS and wondering which of my colleagues now considered me some lowlife misogynist who smacked his wife around, driving her to bizarrely desperate measures. Without anyone saying a word to me, I felt scrutinized at every turn, every look, every conversation. I could imagine the behind the scenes:
"I hear he was a real monster."
"She must have just snapped."
"I guess you never really know people."
"They seemed so normal."
The sane people in my life all cried in unison the same sentiment over and over again: "Even if you hit her, kicked her, pushed her down flights of stairs, it DOES NOT excuse what she did." Consolation factor: zero. I was a stable husband for twelve years. I never hit her or cheated on her. I didn't drink excessively or take drugs and I was a good father to our children. I of course had her on tape admitting all of this. It became my fantasy for everyone we knew to gather around and hear it

at full volume.

Another brand new problem to rival previous brand new problem: walking the halls of DHHS and running into Allison's victims, Zach and Gabe. Zach appeared unfazed by his notoriety. Each time I saw him, he was beaming. He carried himself like a young, confident, popular high school student. All of which he was. But as I watched him, whether he was playing grab ass with his fellow jocks, or flirting with some coy little princess, sometimes just feet from my own classroom, he appeared to have missing parts: shame, humility, discretion. A foolish thought for me to have ever had. To collude with a female teacher in the way that he did shows the polar opposite of shame, humility, and discretion. These sightings were a nightmare. And not just for me. I have to think they must have been horrific for most students to witness. For others, I'm sure it gave them something to tweet about.

Gabe was a different story. Shy and even a bit sullen, he kept a low profile, which must have been a feat for a handsome, well-liked boy. Gabe looked so much like his older brother who was a current student of mine that I often nodded to him in the hall. Moments later would I realize my mistake. This happened often enough for me to want to reach out to him and put him at ease. So I asked his brother one morning if he and Gabe would see me at the end of the day. I admitted it was for the sake of meeting and shaking hands and moving forward.

Gabe did end up coming to my room that same day. He was alone. Putting my hand out towards him, I said it was nice to meet him and I was sorry it wasn't under better circumstances.

"Me too," he said.

"I just want you to know something," I said. "I'm sorry for what you must be going through."

He thanked me. When he was just about to open the door, I said one last thing:

"I just met you, but you're obviously a remarkable kid. I'll never know how you kept this quiet for almost a year."

He seemed to consider this for a moment before he looked at the ground and nodded his head:

"It's because I didn't want all of *this* to happen."

I made a point that day of informing my principal and superintendent that I had met with Gabe. Tom told me he thought clearing the air was a good idea. T.J. disagreed.

"I just wanted to tell him I had no hard feelings," I said.

"I understand."

"It was all of thirty seconds," I said. "And it was a good talk."

T.J. nodded his head, forced a polite smile, and told me to never do it again.

An email was sent off a few days later to the faculty. It was a list of the students who would be attending the Nashville trip in a couple of weeks. Gabe's name was on it. That day, T.J. called me to his office to inform me I would no longer be chaperoning. There was nothing to say, so I thanked him for his time and headed back to my classroom.

Luck was beyond elusive during this time. Emily ended things between us. She sent me a text message telling me she wished to be honest and that she felt things were not working out and good luck. I responded by showing up at her salon with the *Boogie Nights* soundtrack CD I had recently picked up for her. She accepted it, kissed me on the cheek, and said she had to get back to work. What I felt for her didn't come close to resembling love. It was a fling. Nothing more. Yet my beaten heart and brain still registered it as one more loss.

My next few appointments with Jim were similar to the first. He talked too much about himself, gave too much advice, and helped confirm whatever doubts I already had about therapy. The upside was that I could tell my attorney and my family that I was in counseling. We all knew it was more an act of appeasement than a commitment to better myself.

"Try to get something out of the sessions," my mother urged me.

"I'm trying."

"Be open. It'll be good for you."

I wanted to tell her that the more effective therapy for me was through drinking and sex and sleeping pills, that I was nowhere near ready to be demonstrative, especially with a stranger. Yet it felt like I had regressed back to boyhood and was unable to make meaningful life decisions. My credibility felt compromised. My ego was slain and I recognized it would be best if I kept my mouth shut and listened to those around me.

Around this time, I learned that if I wanted my arrest charges dropped that I was to attend a mandatory nine-week Family Violence program in New Haven that would begin in May. The Jekyll and Hyde schizophrenia that was the humor and tragedy of this stipulation made it a favorite topic of conversation among my friends, one of whom said he'd pay me a hundred dollars if I could prove that I wore a wife beater t-shirt to my first class.

One positive: I received a firm date when Allison would be vacating the house. March 20th. Taking that day off of work, I packed my things, cleaned the in-law apartment, and drove to my house for the first time in close to two months. My mother and sister met me at the front door. When we walked inside, I felt a wave of nostalgia sweep over me. Flashing back to when we bought the place just four years earlier, I recalled the elation Allison and I felt over the move to Madison, ready to lay down roots and focus on our family.

My mother and sister and I walked through the house, taking inventory over what was taken and what was left behind. Not much of it was terribly surprising. Allison and I had arranged a list through our attorneys, so I wasn't expecting to see any major deviations. One particularly mawkish touch was a handmade pillow she left in one of the walk-in closets. The pillow, small and pink and gaudy, was not so much left as it was staged. Leaning against the far wall, the pillow boasted, in thin, fancy cursive, *They Lived Happily Ever After.*

I didn't have Robbie and Riley that night. This made it sadder and stranger as I walked the empty rooms, trying to force the feeling of home on myself. It was the eeriest night I had ever lived through. I needed noise. I would have killed for some noise. I craved the sound of cartoons coming from the living room or an argument about the rules of Candyland. Making the best of my solitude, I sat down at my kitchen table, poured a glass of wine from a newly opened bottle, and wrote two things: the foreword to this book and a letter I planned to give each of my neighbors.

Dear Neighbor,

It is with the heaviest heart and nothing but humility that I write this letter. As many of you do not know me, please let me introduce myself. My name is Rob Marchese and I live at --------. I have been a high school teacher here in Madison for the past eleven years. During this time, I have fallen in love with the town, the school, its students, and my job.

The past couple of months have been as harrowing as anything I could have ever imagined. All I can say about the actions of my soon-to-be ex-wife is that she has devastated our family. Words cannot even begin to express the heartache I have endured over what she has done. My aim is not at all to demonize her; I feel her actions speak for themselves - not to mention the way they have adversely affected my family, DHHS, the teaching profession, as well as the town and community.

I have two sweet and gorgeous children, Robbie and Riley, and they have been, and continue to be, my sole focus. They absolutely, unequivocally DO NOT deserve any of this. I will do anything and everything to keep them safe and happy. Part of this entails keeping them in their home and town and school. I therefore hope you will find it in your hearts to understand our plight and to accept us once again as your neighbors.

As far as my own troubles that occurred at the end of January, all I can say is that living in my house with my soon-to-be ex-wife became unbearable. Suffice it to say, what happened now seems like a textbook ending to such an ordeal. Coexisting under such circumstances proved impossible. I hate admitting that I would not have done much differently, but it's the truth.

Please know that all I want is to move forward. And I'd very much like to continue doing so at --------. So please don't be afraid to say hello to me or my children.

Sincerely,

Rob, Robbie, and Riley Marchese

Chapter 6

I made the best of being a single father. Buying new artwork and furniture and bedding, I gave my house a more masculine touch than it had before. Combing through each room, I eliminated all traces of Allison. Photographs. Knick knacks. Pillows. Candles. I moved out of the master bedroom, swapping it for the kids' upstairs rec space. Robbie and Riley approved once they saw how their now bigger playroom was outfitted with a brand new ping pong table, popcorn maker, and gumball machine. For them, though, the piece de resistance was the trampoline I had installed where their mother's garden once stood in the backyard. Maybe I was compensating for loss in a superficial way. Maybe I was buying my children's affection. Maybe I was passively saying "Fuck you" to their mother. Maybe I didn't care how any of it appeared.

Allison ended up moving into a seven hundred square foot duplex two towns away in Branford. I surmised that her notoriety was as much a cause for the difficulty in finding a place as her strained financial situation was.

"How come Mommy has to move?" Riley asked one night over dinner.

I explained to my children that because I was still teaching in Madison that it made sense for me to remain in town. They accepted this. And though it would be financially tight, I was determined to remain in the house once the divorce was finalized. There were reasons for my recalcitrance. Moving would be an acknowledgment of defeat. It would compromise stability for my kids. It would crush the simple dream I had that I would one day see my children walk the halls of the very school in which I taught.

I began to shut the doors to my children's bedrooms when they

114

weren't with me. Yet there were reminders of them at every turn – their school pictures and artwork and toys and DVDs. Doing their laundry could set me off on a crying spree. During this alone time, I would drift aimlessly from room to room, listening to the awful quiet for long stretches before filling it with either violent sobs or else screaming Robbie and Riley's names until my voice gave out. One late Saturday afternoon, I picked up my guitar, strummed a few chords, hummed a melody, and wrote one of my most unaffected songs. It stood behind no barriers or ambiguity. It was as sinewy and lean a song as any I had ever written:

"This Place is Broken"

This place is broken / The proof's right there
It's in her eyes / It's in her stare
This place is broken / Broken everywhere

The clocks are shattered / They're stuck in time
The clocks are broken / Like me and mine
The doors are damaged / The wood is split
The doors are broken / Like all this shit

The bed is burnt-out / The sheets are frayed
The bed is broken / Like promises made
The walls are weathered / There're holes to fill
The walls are broken / Just like my will

This place is broken / The proof's right there
It's in her eyes / It's in her stare
This place is broken / Broken everywhere

The floors are splintered / The boards are bent
The floors are broken / Like time misspent
The songs are over / The music's dead
The songs are broken / And stuck in my head

This house is haunted / Its ghosts set free
This house is broken / For the world to see
This life is over / It's washed ashore
This life is broken / This life's no more

This place is broken / The proof's right there
It's in her eyes / It's in her stare
This place is broken / Broken everywhere

Gone were the family sit-down meals of pork chops and applesauce or salmon and asparagus. Too much work for a single father. I was living on chips and salsa and scrambled eggs. Yet Robbie and Riley were taken care of. They ate well, slept well, and played well. Both continued their progress at school, and both remained carefree kids who wanted only to please their parents.

Bedtime became a brutal ritual. It wrecked me to say goodnight. I felt an obligation to stand guard over them as they slept and ward off possible dreams of a newly broken family. I wanted to massage into their young brains images of the beach and birthdays and being happy and wildly loved. The bedtime stories I had told my children for as long as they could appreciate them began to grow extinct. Robbie, having four years on his sister, was of course a veteran of my absurd adventures starring Goose Boy McCoy – his alias – and an adversary who often had a name like Slothman or Stonefist. For added entertainment, I would toss in a few Scooby Doo characters to accompany Goose Boy on his journey to justice. As for Riley, who was by no means interested in lame tales of unicorns and princesses, I invented the crime fighting duo of Chunk-a-Muffin – her alias – and Magic Guitar Girl.

These stories now seemed like vestiges of a life that was no longer viable. This is not to say I didn't try. I did. Like I had done countless times in the past, I would lie in bed with my children, holding them close to me, kissing them all over their faces, all the while conjuring up an anecdote that would amuse and stimulate their brains before bed. But nothing came, so I didn't force it. It suited all of us to simply be together, wading through the foreignness of the moment.

•   •   •   •   •

On May 5th, I began attending my mandatory Domestic Violence classes in New Haven. The sessions, which ran from 6:30–8:00, were at the Consultation Center on Whitney Avenue. They were overseen by two Family Relations Counselors, Alan, a scrawny, middle-aged Norwegian man with a bony, narrow face, and Alisha, a young, gorgeous black woman with a perfect smile and just the right temperament to deal with a room full of thugs. The group, which had thirteen members, all male, all between the ages of twenty and fifty, wore enough do-rags and tattoos to rival a band of pirates. With my curly brown hair, black-framed glasses, and Polo shirts, I must have looked ridiculous among them. Sitting at a large conference table under harsh fluorescent lights in a windowless room, we must have appeared like some reject corporation about to discuss some ill-fated merger.

A set of class rules was given on that first day.

Rule 1. Arrive on time and remain for the entire class; the front door will lock at 6:40.

Rule 2. Be respectful in waiting area.

Rule 3. You are expected to attend eight of the nine class sessions.

Rule 4. Disruptive behavior before, during, or after class will not be tolerated.

Rule 5. Childcare is not provided.

Rule 6. You are expected to take part in class discussions and complete any coursework and/or homework.

Rule 7. All electronic devices must remain off and out of sight during each class session.

Rule 8. Sunglasses are not allowed to be worn during class sessions.

Rule 9. You are expected to be free from alcohol and drugs when attending the program.

Rule 10. Share air time – let others speak.

Rule 11. Be alert and attentive.

I'm sure like the rest of the group, I felt I did not belong there. I was not a violent derelict with a track record of abusing my wife or any woman for that matter. My mind was thus made up to follow the tenets put forth by Stickboy and Black Beauty, but to otherwise get nothing out of the sessions. On that first day, we listened to our hosts talk about the program before we were asked to introduce ourselves and share our story. When it came to me, I inhaled a bit before straightening myself in my seat. Then I offered up a single sentence:

"My name is Rob," I said, offering a long pause before I thought of what else to say. "And I've recently discovered that I married the wrong person."

This aroused faint laughter from the group. Even Alan smiled a little. Alisha offered me a sympathetic look. When it seemed evident that I was done speaking, Alan asked if I had more to add. I thought about it for a moment. The truth is that I could have dominated that entire hour and a half with my twisted little tale; it would have been effortless to work myself into a fit while doing so. It's likely that I would have elicited easy sympathy from my new cohorts. Yet I declined to speak any further. Turning my attention to the next man at the table, I sighed a little, knowing that my time at the Consultation Center over these next many weeks would hasten the alien feelings that had already taken over my body.

•   •   •   •   •

Whether it was the change in season or my renewed domestic stability, I began playing more music around this time. I even began to sit in regularly with a friend's band at The Bee & Thistle, a B&B they played in Old Lyme. The Bee was a far cry from most of the dives I was used to. There was art on the walls, collars on the waitstaff, and locks on the restroom doors. Overseeing all of this was the manager, a busty, tattooed twenty-nine-year-old named Tosh who asked me to have a drink with her one night after a gig. I accepted and we met at a dive bar called The Monkey Farm in Old Saybrook. We ordered food and beer and talked about music and literature. After a few more drinks, she asked if I wanted to go back to her place. I again accepted. We took my car. On the way, she told me she loved that I played the harmonica.

118

"Why is that?"

"It just makes a girl curious as to what else you can do with that mouth of yours."

Tosh appeared as though at a moment's notice she might hurl herself comfortably into a Quentin Tarantino film where she would say things that lived between being pseudo-poetic and just downright absurd. She drank and smoked and flirted and referred to herself as "Mama" and knew everyone and hugged them and called them "doll" in a pretend European accent. She was covered in ornate tattoos of flowers, stars, and vines, not to mention random holes all over her body from old piercings that would never fully heal. She pointed out to me that she looked like Elizabeth Taylor. I didn't argue.

Tosh's place turned out to be the one she shared with her grandparents. This proved a less than ideal setting for our future gatherings. So we began to play house in Madison when Robbie and Riley were staying with their mother.

"Mama loves it here, baby doll," she'd say while making a pitcher of pina coladas, "loves it, loves it, loves it."

We were having a fine time together, ordering take-out and getting drunk and listening to music and playing Scrabble. I felt like I was back in college and Tosh was the wild party-girl while I was the R.A. She would sit on my front porch and smoke and tell me about the tattoos she was saving for or an idea she had about turning the basement of The Bee & Thistle into an after-hours speakeasy. Whenever she brought up Robbie and Riley, whose pictures were hanging throughout the house, she'd be sure to mention how good she was with children and how they so often adored her. This was easy to see. She was animated, spirited, and quite clever. Yet I was nowhere near ready to have Robbie and Riley meet her. We were just learning how to exist as a trio, how to live in our house once again after my long absence, how to cope with only seeing each other fifty percent of the time, and I wanted to establish a rhythm to these things before bringing in an outsider.

Allison saw things differently. Months prior, Robbie and Riley had begun telling me about a man named Jeremy they were seeing quite frequently. They told me he was Mommy's boss. It was *Jeremy* this and

119

Jeremy that. *Jeremy* took them out for dinner. *Jeremy* took them to a Red Sox game. *Jeremy* liked the Grateful Dead. Through our financial affidavit disclosures, I knew where Allison worked, so I was able to do a little research on this Jeremy. Putting aside his bloated cartoonish appearance, as well as the fact that he was willingly dating someone in Allison's position, it infuriated me that my children were in the company of this stranger. Each time his name came out of their mouths, I had to brace myself and refrain from losing my cool.

Within a few weeks of their dating, he was spending the night at her Branford apartment with my children present. Before long, they were all spending nights – sometimes entire weekends – at his place in Waterford. I received news that Jeremy's parents babysat Robbie and Riley while their son and Allison went to a concert. I received news that the kids shared a hot tub with Allison and Jeremy. I received news that Jeremy was bad mouthing me in front of them. In just a few months, I heard more Jeremy stories than I could count. Knowing her affinity for male attention, I was not at all surprised that Jeremy had become Allison's lifeline.

"He's always around," Robbie would tell me. "Why does he have to *always* be around?"

This had become some formulaic TV movie where the parents split up and the children are introduced to an outsider who rivals either mom or dad. Rumors fly, tensions build, confrontation becomes inevitable. Jeremy struck me as a lonely slob who saw an easy opportunity to sleep with a vulnerable woman in major crisis mode, but he was obviously stable enough to keep his hands off my kids. I was therefore left with the single option of listening to these maddening stories and embracing the fact that I was powerless to change a thing.

A few variables emboldened Allison around this time. One was Jeremy. Another were the few supporters who stood by her. Yet another was when she had family visiting. Her parents would work in shifts, coming to stay with her for a week at a clip, usually when she had a looming court appearance. These support systems offered her the platform to not only deny responsibility for her actions, but to redirect the focus on me.

She and I would engage in text threads that saw her expound on how I maligned her family during our marriage, how I didn't kiss her enough on the mouth, how I spent too much time writing or playing music, how I loved our children more than her. Sometimes I would respond. Other times I would not. Making her see what she had done, its severity, and probable outcome, was futile.

"You molested teenage boys," I wrote to her in one thread. "There's nothing to justify this. Nothing."

"I was lonely."

"So go to a bar and have an affair with someone your own age."

"I would never do that."

"You say that with pride. Yet you have no problem turning to pedophilia."

"I did not turn to pedophilia."

"Yes you did. And that's what you'll forever be: a pedophile."

"I am not a pedophile."

"You are. And your pathetic vanity destroyed our family."

This ended the thread. It was always this way – whenever I bluntly stated my truth, and did so with caustic indifference, she would retreat with silence of her own.

In another thread, I accused her of putting her own needs above Robbie's and Riley's. This was typical behavior, I pointed out. Then I made a dig that she had nothing and no one and how she should thus have ample time for parenting.

"I do too have friends."

"This is your concern after I tell you that I think you're a neglectful parent? Proving to me that you have friends?"

"Well, I do."

"What you have is a few relationships born out of *desperation* on your part, and *pity* on theirs. Enjoy."

End of thread. Nothing left to say. From either of us. Yet this particular exchange caused me to consider her few supporters. I was nonplussed over their existence.

"It's insane," I would say to my family. "Completely insane. Are these people blind?"

"Look at it this way," my mother said, "even Charles Manson had followers."

"I suppose."

"Some people are busybodies. They need a project."

"It makes no sense."

"Just remember what you *can* control and what you *can't*."

My mother's wisdom around this time was beginning to infuriate me. I craved talks about injustice and revenge. Nothing more.

Meanwhile, my weekly sessions at New Haven's Consultation Center were becoming spectacles unto themselves. The cast of characters was rock solid. There was the Mumbler. He was a muscle-bound twenty-something with wire-rimmed glasses who had a lot to say, but barely 10% was ever audible. There was the Pessimist. He was a cranky, put-upon complainer who often announced how the sessions were nothing but a con job, a money making scam, a farce, all perpetrated by the government. There was the Philosopher. He looked to be the youngest in the group. Trying so hard to say profound things, he always ended up overstating the obvious and wasting a lot of time. There was the Victim, the Gangster, the Mensch, the Milquetoast, and of course, the extras.

I was among this latter group. Though I kept silent, I made it my business to keep upright posture, polite eye contact, and a composed demeanor. All I wanted was June 30th to arrive. My final class. Then I would be done.

But something happened during that sixth session on June 9th. Alisha, looking at me with her dark, gorgeous eyes, commented that the group didn't hear enough from Rob. Weeks had gone by and Rob was often silent. And wouldn't we all like to hear from Rob. It's a testament to her skills that she did not come across as challenging when she said this. There was a sense of real concern in her voice.

"All we know about you is that you feel you've married the wrong person," she said.

All eyes were on me. Strangers' eyes. Expecting me to do what? Open up? Reveal my inner demons? What would it get me? It would fill the time is all. Maybe a minute or two at the most. They would listen to a foreign voice discuss problems that were not theirs, nod their heads, and count down until 8:00. Yet something compelled me to speak. I'm not sure if it was because a beautiful woman wanted something from me and I didn't want to disappoint her, or because I needed to purge something, anything, and so why not here and why not now. I told them that my wife had cheated on me. That I was humiliated and hurt and disgusted.

"It's hard to know what to do with all of that, isn't it?" asked Alisha. "A good start is to open up about it. Talk it through. Listen to the sound of your voice say how it is you feel."

Then silence. No one else offered up anything. I wasn't sure if we were moving on to someone else, or if I was to continue.

"Maybe I should turn my tragedy into art," I said. "Maybe put together a stand up bit on what she did. Put a positive spin on the whole thing."

A few interested faces. They seemed to sense that I had more to say.

"That might be therapeutic," I added. "To make light of the situation. I'll go on a national tour. I'll call it the Whore Tour."

That was all it took. The group erupted in laughter. Even Alan and Alisha cracked a couple of grins.

"Do you know what recently dawned on me?" I asked no one in particular. "That we test children for all sorts of conditions when they're in utero. But why are we not testing our spouses before we marry them? We should give them the Rorschach test to see if they're insane. 'What does this look like?' 'What does that look like?' 'A penis?' 'Sorry, you fail.' The test could even be renamed in honor of my wife: They could call it the Ror*cock* test."

It took a few minutes for the hysterics to subside. I suppose I lucked out that the facilitators of the group had also been amused. I was, after all, in direct violation of Rule 4. Disruptive behavior before, during, or after class will not be tolerated. Humor aside, I had opened up to a roomful of strangers, and was pleasantly surprised just how cathartic it turned out to be.

123

• • • • •

Tosh eventually learned the details of my situation. She was talking to some officious housewife during an exercise class one morning when my name came up. Not exactly an ideal way to find out, but it did manage to remove the burden from my shoulders.

"What do you think?" I asked her one evening as we sat outside the Bee & Thistle.

"I think it's a fucking nightmare."

"For sure it is."

"I was speechless for five minutes after I heard the story. And you know me. Just try and get Mama to shut her pie hole."

Lighting a cigarette, Tosh launched into some sincerity. She told me she couldn't imagine going through something like this. She had respect and admiration, she said, for how I managed to endure. She knew nothing about my screaming fits and the sleeping pills and how I had to anesthetize myself with wine just so I could fall asleep half the time. She didn't know what my insides looked like, how they were hurt and hollow and how my organs were probably withering away to nothing. Her ignorance couldn't be helped. Everything she said flew in the face of being a twenty-nine-year-old party girl. She was full of more warmth and wisdom and compassion than I knew what to do with.

Tosh and I continued our relationship through the spring and into summer. Our intimacy transcended the physical. Offsetting her wildness with a great deal of depth, she shared with me stories of her own past. There was abuse and addiction and abandonment. Many of these tales could rival anything I had ever been through. She asked about meeting Robbie and Riley. She asked about moving in with me. She asked if I ever considered marrying again. With all of her confidence and savvy and femininity, she managed to cope quite well with my very disappointing answers.

• • • • •

As the school year was winding down, new district jobs for 2015-2016 were being posted. One of them was to replace Allison. Because I was the Coordinator of the English Department, the task fell on me. I thus devised a committee, wrote up some questions, and scheduled the interviews. Though none of my colleagues said a word about it, they must have all felt, as we sat in a semicircle around one candidate at a time, like we were enacting a scene from a Kafka novel.

What was equally surreal was having to walk into Allison's old classroom. Room 347. It was a place where I used to sneak a kiss during her planning period. Or pay her a visit with the purpose of teasing her in front of her students. Sometimes she and I would have lunch alone in her room and talk about Robbie and Riley or just commiserate over a coworker who was driving us mad. Now I wanted the room quarantined. Sealed off. In my mind it was tantamount to the scene of a massacre.

The school year was winding down. I would be glad to see it go, but summer would be tricky. I had grown accustomed to having that time off with my wife and children. Not that we were jet setters who would vacation in Belize or Saint Croix, but the couple of months we shared was invaluable for raising two children so close to the beach in a tight knit community where we both taught. I could hardly wait until I no longer had to grade another essay or look at another journal. My teaching, naturally, was shit, and had been shit since my return back in January. I was far too ravaged to put any real time into my lessons; most of my energy was consumed by going through the motions as best I could. The last piece I happened to teach one of my American Lit. classes was John Updike's story "A&P." It only dawned on me about halfway through the class that this was the same story I taught to get the job at DHHS. As luck would have it, the story once again proved powerful; I'm convinced, the same way I was eleven years earlier when I first taught "A&P," that it had to do with the story's final line: "...and my stomach kind of fell as I felt how hard the world was going to be to me hereafter." This was a group of smart students, but there's no way they could have grasped the timeliness, the momentum, or the personal gravity of those words.

•   •   •   •   •

I hadn't seen Allison in months, since a mutual court appearance with our attorneys. But as Robbie's baseball season began, we were forced to see one another at his games, which were held at The Surf Club's athletic fields. If it was my weekend with the kids, I would bring them to the game. She would do the same on her weekends. With her iced coffee and Ray-Bans, she gave off the appearance of the quintessential Madison mom who had come to cheerlead for her son and his team.

She and I set up our chairs at least fifty or so feet from one another and did our best to avoid eye contact. Riley, who attended each of her big brother's games, would simply run back and forth and share her time with both Mom and Dad.

One particular Saturday in early June saw flawless weather. The day was mild and sunny and stood as the perfect harbinger for the upcoming summer. The magnificent blue sky loomed overhead. The horizon had streaks of burnt orange and red spiraling through a few low hanging clouds. To my surprise, Allison was nowhere to be found. I was therefore left alone to cheer for Robbie while playing tag with his little sister. This lasted to the third inning when Allison showed up, wearing what looked like her work clothes, casual attire befitting her minimum wage job at FTD, a floral delivery service out of Centerbrook, CT. As she walked towards the field, she took intermittent glances over her shoulder. I noticed a subtle change in how she carried herself. There was a nervousness in her face, and her posture was less upright. Walking past me and Riley, she put her head down and found a spot to stand by the third base line. After a few moments, she took out her phone and studied the screen for a bit. This lasted for a minute until she called for our daughter to come see her. Riley did so and they hugged and kissed before Allison gathered herself and walked towards the parking lot. When my daughter found her way back to me, she said the very thing that happened to be on my mind:

"Mommy didn't even say hello to Robbie."

This behavior was explained when she texted me a half hour later:

"Please tell Robbie I'm sorry I missed him, but there was an incident in the parking lot: I was assaulted by Gabe's family when they spotted me walking towards the field."

If I cared enough to respond, I would have said "What the fuck did you expect? With the way you've paraded around town these last many months – it's about time someone confronted you. You've thought nothing about going to Cumberland Farms and Bradley and Wall and Schoolhouse Deli. You deserve to be accosted. And I'm glad you were. I hope it was humiliating."

An hour later, she sent a second text:

"I know you hate me, but I'm a little hurt you haven't reached out to see if I'm okay."

My eyes must have bulged from their sockets over this message. Yet all I could do was take a screenshot of it and send it to my mother and sister.

•　　　•　　　•　　　•　　　•

June 30th arrived. The school year was over, dead to me, a charred heap of ash. My final Family Violence class would conclude at 8:00 p.m. that evening. Graduation day.

Excerpts of a movie were shown during that last session at the Consultation Center. It was a New Zealand film called *Once Were Warriors*. The story centers around the domestic hazards that ensue over poverty, abuse, and alcoholism in an urban family. It was the final class and I was determined to open myself to inspiration and insight. I didn't want to leave, after a nine-week investment, without having gained an ounce of enlightenment. So with absolute focus, I sat upright as the lights dimmed and the DVD began. But the film, which is low budget and poorly acted, might as well have been science fiction; it didn't depict any problems that ever plagued my life or marriage. Allison and I didn't struggle with violence or finances or booze.

Once the clips were shown, a rowdy dialogue began. This must have pleased Stickboy and Black Beauty, both of whom were leading the discussion. They had cherry-picked this very movie, knowing it would resonate with this group. Looking around the room, I discovered that even some of the other extras, my own brethren, men who usually spoke little and kept to themselves, now had much to say. And even though I was happy that the sessions were over in a matter of minutes, and that I would never see these people again, I was still struck by the loneliness of my ordeal.

When the session ended, there were hoots and hollers as the group wasted no time in heading towards the parking lot and back to their lives. I remained in my seat, waiting to see if relief would wash over me. Nothing happened. Alisha was gathering some papers and straightening up when she spotted me.

"How are you feeling now that it's over?"

"The exact same."

"Well, I'm happy for you now that you're done."

"I'm sorry I was so useless."

"Don't be silly."

"I think my story may be a bit different from everyone else's."

She nodded her head.

"I know how that sounds," I went on, "but believe me, it is."

"What makes you feel that way?"

Taking a seat next to me, she folded her hands in her lap and smiled. She smelled like fresh flowers and apricot. I wriggled in my chair before turning to Alisha and explaining what my wife had done to our family. I left nothing out. Her expression vacillated between sorrow and concern. By the time I had finished talking, Alisha agreed that my story did appear to stand on its own.

"What do you think led up to these circumstances?"

"How much time do you have?"

She shrugged her shoulders and pointed out that class was over and that she had nowhere to be.

"Talk," she said. "Go ahead."

The starting point was obvious to me. Chicago. I told Alisha how I had moved there with my friend Matt when we were in our twenties. Aimless and hungry for adventure, I quit grad school at the University of Hartford and broke the news to my parents that I was leaving

Connecticut, unsure if I would ever return. They were circumspect over my tenuous plans, yet bid me an emotional farewell. Once there, I made barely an impression upon the city. I worked in a little breakfast spot in Lincoln Park and spent most of my time writing a shitty screenplay and trying to put together a decent band. Both endeavors proved to be quiet failures. Yet I did manage to fall head over heels in love with a gorgeous young actress named Tracey. It was Tracey, three years my junior, who gave me direction and inspiration. She was the first girl I knew who could stomach Neil Young, and I could turn her on to esoteric films and e.e. cummings and sex with the lights on. Within the year, her blind ambition to experience the halcyon days of her own youth got the better of us. By the time I returned to Connecticut, I was as directionless as ever. Searching the classifieds one morning, I learned of a teaching position at Grove, a therapeutic boarding school in Madison. I got the job, which turned my life around. The kids who attended Grove were disturbed and intense. It proved the perfect fit.

After close to two years, I met a Canadian intern named Allison whom I began dating. There were many casual flings prior to Allison, but this was the first girl who made me forget about Tracey. Allison built me up. Tracey leveled me and Allison cradled the pieces and carefully reconstructed them. There were some red flags for sure – she volunteered tales of her promiscuity as well as her volatile relationships with her parents – but I might have been blinded by what I thought was genuine adoration she felt for me. We married in the summer of 2002, in Canada, and then settled into a life together. We bought a modest home in Clinton, CT, and each left Grove to eventually work as English teachers at Daniel Hand High School. The rhythm of our domestic and professional life eventually gave way to some concerning behaviors I began to witness regularly. Jealousy. Vanity. Rage. Insecurity. The target for Allison's angst was her family and her upbringing. Her mother, she argued, was manic. Her father, an alcoholic and ex-con, was even more so. Even her younger siblings received scrutiny. According to Allison, they were spoiled and entitled and they enabled her mother's hostilities.

There was a great deal of relief she felt over having moved several hundred miles away. Yet there was crippling guilt as well. It was this erraticism that began to dominate our life together. Her family did little to help. They mocked her American husband and her American home and whatever ideals were not steeped in the conventions of their beloved Canada. When Allison revealed to her mother that she was in counseling and had begun taking Prozac, the reaction was brutal.

"She's fearful that I'll expose her abuse," Allison would say. "All she cares about is appearances. It's so sad."

Encouraging her therapy, I tried to provide as much stability as I could. This meant starting a family. Our son was born on July 29, 2007. We named him Robert Christopher Marchese. A chubby, bright-eyed baby, Robbie was an excuse to brag, to stay home, to go out and show him off, to revisit those salient memories I had of childhood and my relationship with my own parents, to contemplate long and hard about not only the future, but how my job as one its architects was suddenly that much more important. My son and I bonded like our lives depended on it. There would be no other way. I knew my competition was stiff: It's the mother this and the mother that, especially in the first year or so. I accepted these terms. Understood them. Hell, I welcomed them. But I wasn't about to take some secondary role. It would have been unnatural for me to do so.

Hindsight has shown me that I was a natural father. Not that I wasn't nervous about Robbie's ear infections, or paranoid about SIDS, and I know I complained about a lack of sleep and free time, but I found myself immersed in the role of parenthood with a kind of euphoria that lived in a brand new light behind my pupils. I felt it. And I knew others could sense it. My parents and my sister and my friends – and Allison, who was equally invested in motherhood. The love and devotion she had for Robbie was evident.

"I love this stage," she would often say, cradling his infant body to her breast.

This became a staple saying of hers. So much so that I suspected she feared Robbie would grow and she would soon be obsolete. There's no doubt that she was integral that first year. And she knew this. Yet I'm certain that the thought of future stages seemed less appealing to her; there would be more work necessary to earn the child's affections.

By the time Robbie turned three, he and his mother were constantly at odds. Her neuroses had reached new heights. Robbie pounced on this. His refusal to obey her, nap for her, wear the outfits she had laid out for him, or even gravitate to her when he needed comfort, caused a gulf in our marriage. I told her she needed to be more tolerant, more relaxed, that Robbie sensed her anxiousness and was either put off by it or capitalized on it. I was accused of segregating her and forming an alliance with our three-year-old.

"I bet you love it," she exclaimed one evening after we put our boy to bed. "Love it that he won't listen to me and is so disrespectful."

"Are you joking?"

"It's 'Daddy this' and 'Daddy that.'"

The truth is that I derived no satisfaction over my son's preference for me at this point. I regarded it for what it was: a stage. I may have thrived on the closeness, but not at my wife's expense. All it did was make me feel sorry for her. She couldn't conceive of tactics to manipulate a small child into obedience, and I found this maddening.

Allison's answer to this was to begin negotiations for a second child.

"I think we should wait," I said.

"For what?"

"For things to settle a bit."

"What does that mean?"

"I just don't think we're ready."

"*You* might not be ready, but I *am*."

My response to her ignorance was to string the matter along for an indeterminate amount of time. The truth is that thoughts of a second baby kept me up at night. I was in love with the idea of another child, particularly a little girl. A playmate for Robbie. Someone to call him Big Brother. Another sweet, gorgeous face to look at and ponder my own meaning and worth. Yet the tumult it would likely cause was plain for me to see. Double the stress. Double the anxiety. Double the unrest. Double the arguments.

One evening after Robbie had fallen asleep, Allison, in a hysterical tantrum, threatened me with divorce.

"I didn't sign up for this," she said.

Each of those six words was a stick of dynamite. I arranged them before me, in the air, in my head, on the tip of her tongue, wondering what might possibly ignite their fuses.

"You didn't sign up for this?"

"No, I didn't."

"This perfect son of ours, this house, our jobs and security and family and friends and future and this life we have together: That's not enough?"

"No, it's not," she said, looking me directly in the eyes.

It might have been harsh and hurtful, but it was also the truth. I was certain of it. She meant what she said. I listened for the hiss of those fuses. I listened with as much clarity as I could achieve. The moment was still and shocking and as real as the three-year-old flesh and blood in the bedroom down the hall. I listened. What I ended up hearing was the sound of my own voice. And I'm positive it shocked both of us equally:

"Okay. We'll have another child. We can try whenever you're ready."

Riley was born on July 9th, 2011. She won me over the second I laid eyes on her. It's not that I forgot my misgivings – I did not – but the love I had for my newborn daughter made any obstacle seem trivial. In this way, I wondered if my wife had been correct all along. Perhaps I was just a selfish prick, a short-sighted Neanderthal whose thinking was base and philosophies specious. It turned out that my instincts were in fact fair. Whatever woes Allison and I shared were not at all assuaged with this addition to our family.

Yet Riley was such a joy, and I had fallen so madly in love with her, that I soon discovered I was nearly complacent when it came to my marriage. My energies were devoted to being a father – so much so that arguing with Allison nearly fell by the wayside. Once fairly stubborn when it came to getting my licks in, I began to resign to the notion that I was no longer as interested in being right, or even heard.

Alisha proved to be a good listener. Her attention was unwavering. This didn't stop me from checking in with her when it dawned on me how long I had been talking. I stated the obvious, that she was under no obligation to sit and listen to a stranger pour out his guts.

"I don't mind," she said. "You've honestly piqued my interest."

This gave me the confidence to continue. I talked about how Allison and I moved around a lot, up and down the shoreline, buying and selling homes every few years. And the shopping. There was no way I could leave out the shopping. This became the sole pastime we had between us. Some couples travel or exercise or bowl or drink together. Allison and I shopped. Constantly. Having children might have slowed us down, but we were undeterred, dragging them to every mall and outlet store in the state. These pastimes, as they turned out to be - the moving, the shopping - seemed born out of some innate restlessness that plagued our marriage.

Once Riley was out of diapers and running amok, Allison began to experience the same sort of ennui she did a few years earlier. She made no attempt to hide what was on her mind: herself. So began her fitness regimen. She had been active since we met, teaching cardio kickboxing classes in town, lifting the occasional weight, and even dabbling in CrossFit. In time, she would start what became a cultish devotion to fine tuning her body.

"Time to lose this baby weight," she'd tell me. "I'm tired of looking like a *mom*."

While I encouraged her discipline - she soon began working out six to seven days a week - my response was to state the obvious: that she in fact *was* a mom. Shaking her head at me, she'd explain that women don't want it to appear as though they have children. A lecture would ensue on how men become sexier as they age, while women did not. Wrinkles, gray hair, the detriments of gravity: These all touched men in very forgiving ways. Women, on the other hand, had a fight on their hands that she claimed I would never truly grasp.

"Ever since we had the kids," she told me one evening, "the boys at school are so much less flirty. Sometime they even call me *mom*."

I kept silent for a few moments to see if she would be struck by her own words. She was not. I told her to get in shape for herself and for her own peace of mind, and for no one and nothing else.

"I know," she'd say, appeasing me, "you're right."

In the summer of 2014, she ran nearly every day, sometimes three or four miles, sometimes up to ten. It was possible for her to be gone for hours at a time. Prior to each run, she'd shower and shave and perfume her body. Two things began to happen. The first one is that the results of her running were evident almost immediately.

"You look great," I told her time and time again.

"Thanks," she'd say, standing in front of the full length mirror on her closet door.

She became taut and muscular and her belly flattened out and it even showed in her face. There was no doubt that her body responded well to whatever she was putting it through.

The second thing that happened is that I became exhausted by what I recognized as unadulterated OCD. The truth is that Allison could do next to nothing in moderation. Whether it had to do with how she folded her clothes, wore her hair, or prepared her food, she was often fixated on the minutiae of her compulsions. She would not only run, but she would talk about her runs, chronicle them on Facebook, plan our days and evenings around them. It became evident that these runs were not merely physical feats that helped her achieve a better body or healthier outlook. They were appearances. She was manufacturing a moment that would allow her to be seen by countless observers: students, parents, friends, colleagues, even strangers. Upon her return home, she made sure to tell me how many horns honked or hands waved while she maneuvered her way through busy downtown Madison in her spandex shorts and sports bra.

One sunny morning, minutes prior to leaving the house, she offered an idea of which she appeared prideful. With an earnest smile and voice, she asked if the kids and I might like to get in the car and drive beside her while she ran. My expression had to have betrayed my agitation when I declined her proposal before heading outside to mow the lawn.

A few weeks during the summer of 2014 might now be counted a landmark stretch of time. Allison was paid to work with Daniel Hand High School's football team on pre-season conditioning drills. The coaches put her front and center of the team where she could take in a panoramic view of what she had at her disposal, which would have been obvious to anyone who learned of this arrangement: sweaty, eager, horny teenage boys. These sessions, which ran for an hour or so during summer hell week, added a full blown addition to her ego, replete with delusions of grandeur that she would somehow be integral to another winning season for the Tigers.

Absurd but nonetheless relevant aside: Former WWF star Bob Backlund showed up at DHHS during one of these summer sessions, while Tony Dorsett, former NFL running back, showed up at another. Both, according to Allison, couldn't get enough of her. They spoke with her about how fit she was, flattered her on her physique, and even offered to meet up with her for one-on-one workouts. Regardless of the veracity, these stories must have been brought up a dozen times that summer. My indifference prompted the comeback from Allison that I was jealous. I told her I was not. I told her I was fed up.

I left Alisha with a few anecdotes. One was about a trip Allison and I took that summer to the Outer Banks. Renting a house with my family, we settled down for a week of eating, drinking, and swimming at the beach, which was just across the street. On the third day, my father pulled me aside after breakfast to ask about his daughter-in-law:

"What's with the cell phone?" he said.

"What are you talking about?"

"She's on the thing constantly."

"I know she is."

"It's a little rude."

"It goes way beyond rude."

"What's she doing on it?"

"Instagram. Yik Yak. Facebook. Snapchat."

My father's forehead became furrowed. I shrugged. Never once did I check my wife's phone. Naively, I suspected she was communicating with her sisters and friends from Canada.

"Do you ever say anything to her about it?" he asked.

What a question. I didn't know where to begin. Sparing him the details, I said I was aware it was a problem and that I would continue to address it, but that I was anything but optimistic. At the end of the trip, during our drive home, I mentioned her phone usage, which had become an all too familiar conversation. Scoffing a little, Allison changed the subject to sex. After a minute or so, she announced that she would be okay if I ever decided to cheat on her. Her only stipulation was that I keep the affair to myself. Her knowing about it, she reasoned, would only complicate matters. I looked in the rearview mirror at Robbie and Riley; they were watching *Rio 2* on the DVD player and had no idea what grownup matters were being discussed.

"Very generous of you," I said.

"I think so."

There seemed to be no punchline to this exchange. I knew she meant what she had said and it left me speechless. Her own jealousy, after all, could be epic. Nothing more was said about her cell phone or offer for me to cheat. We drove on in silence, putting the south in our rearview mirror, both of us unaware that this trip was to mark the last vacation we would ever take together.

A sturdy companion to the tech piece was that Allison had become interested in pornography. The routine that developed involved her slinking into our bedroom with her computer and a sheepish grin on her face. Locking the door behind her, she could be in there for up to an hour. This routine became steadfast to the point where she began buying toys to accompany her. We spoke little of her new habit. All she offered was an apology for not inviting me to participate.

"It's like when you write," she said. "You do it alone."

"Interesting comparison."

Another development was how she began to dress. She spent hundreds that summer and fall on an almost entirely new wardrobe. This included countless skirts, backless dresses, heels, boots, and blouses so form fitting that you could make out the definition of her arms through the fabric.

"You look like you're going to a Hollywood premier," I would tell her, "not to room 347 to teach *Hamlet*."

Her defense was to remind me of how many compliments she received on daily basis. On her body. On her clothes. On her fitness routines.

"I still say it's inappropriate."

"Well, I say it's not."

"No other female teacher dresses like this. Not one. Look around."

"Why don't you just worry about yourself," she'd tell me.

One morning Allison visited my classroom while I was in the middle of a lesson. She wore a white blouse tucked into a tight fitting black shirt, high heels, and a coyness that might have been obvious only to those who knew her well. With no qualms about interrupting, she made her way to the front of the room and asked me about what I had packed for our lunches that day. Her eyes veered off in the direction of my class as she shifted her body weight ever so slightly from side to side. Pausing at the randomness of her inquiry, I examined my students' expressions to see if they understood what was happening. I'm confident they did not. At best, they were mildly amused and appreciative over the interruption. Later that day, I asked Allison into my room where I admonished her behavior.

"You're kidding, right?" she said, a smug grin creeping across her face.

"I'm *not* kidding. We both know what you were doing and I want it to stop. It's bad enough with the way you dress, but now you're making guest appearances in front of my students."

Blushing a little, she rolled her eyes and denied the accusation. Folding my arms across my chest, I stood my ground without saying another word. Allison and I looked at one another for a few moments before she gathered herself and headed back to her room. The guest appearances ended that day. The inappropriate attire did not.

I left Alisha with one final story about my marriage. It was about a DHHS football game Allison and I attended with our children in the fall of 2014. The story was a good place for me to end my narrative – and for no reason other than to draw attention to a single statement that ended up being disturbingly prophetic.

We brought the kids to the last home game of the 2014 season. It was a couple of weeks before Thanksgiving. Crisp night air. Clear, star-studded sky. The four of us were wearing hats and gloves and heavy coats. Robbie and Riley were sipping hot chocolate and being fawned over by DHHS students. The crowd, the energy, the brilliance of the stadium lights, all transformed a New England high school football game into a scene that could have taken place in Southlake, Texas.

Allison took Riley, just three at the time, up to the bleachers to watch the Tigers. Robbie and I went for a walk. We made a trip to the concession stand where we bought Starbursts and Ring Pops. We found a Nerf game with some of his school friends where we worked on his spiral. We eventually made our way back to the girls. As we moved past the visitor section and headed towards the Madison side, I could see Allison standing on the riser that hovered directly over the team. Her coat and hat were off and she was holding Riley, who had grown tired and looked like a limp doll in her mother's arms. I slowed my pace and watched them from afar. I could see that Allison was talking to some of the players below. Her attention never drifted from her subjects. I watched her smile and laugh and toss her head back to clear the hair from her eyes. On occasion, she would bounce our near sleeping daughter or rub her back. In plain view, and yet with the furtiveness of a private eye, I walked towards them both while I held my son's hand.

When I was probably thirty feet away, I could see who she was talking to: three fully suited, sidelined boys who held their helmets by the facemasks and swung them in the air as they stared up at their pretty teacher. The swells of cheering fans made it impossible to hear what was being said, even as Robbie and I grew closer to them. Allison's focus on the boys was unwavering. Even when we were within a few feet, she didn't seem to have peripheral vision. Robbie and I stood there, waiting to be acknowledged. Then one of the players looked in my direction and said hello.

As we took our children to sit on the bleachers, I was processing what I had just witnessed. To a casual onlooker, it may have seemed innocuous – a friendly exchange between students and their teacher. Nothing more. But it struck me in an unsettling way. My stomach felt knotty and the taste of the cold air was suddenly bitter. I stared at my wife who was holding our now sleeping daughter.

"What was *that?*" I asked.

"What was *what?*"

Her attention was on the game.

"That exchange."

"It's called a conversation."

"Is that what it was?"

Our voices blended in with the crowd. We kept our attention on the field as we spoke. Robbie asked if we would be leaving soon. I told him we would after the halftime show. Then, digging through my gut for something to say to my wife, something that captured my feeling that her conversation with the boys meant more to her than it should have, that it had with it the excitement and danger of shooting a gun for the first time, I managed to come up with a single sentence I said practically in a whisper that only she could hear:

"We're going to read about you in the paper one of these days."

She glared at me through dark, hardened eyes, but said nothing. She seemed to be considering my insult, or maybe working on a comeback, or maybe contemplating something so private and possibly hellish that it spooked even her. After a moment, she stood up, collected her coat and hat, and with our daughter in her arms, headed towards the parking lot.

Nearly an hour had passed since I had begun telling Alisha my story. She barely moved in that time. When I reminded her of my view that I had married the wrong person, she said it didn't appear that simple to her.

"Why not?" I asked.

"I'm not sure."

"Just know that I gave you the highlights," I told her. "There's more."

"I'm trying to process everything you've just told me. There's hardly anything I can say in response that will seem appropriate right now."

"I understand."

"For starters, it's quite a story."

"I suppose it is."

"And I'm sorry that happened to you and your family."

"So am I."

"But I still don't think it's as easy as saying you married the wrong person."

She swiveled in her chair and took a moment to formulate her thought.

"Who knows why it went wrong, or when it did, or how it could have possibly been saved? I don't think it'll help to dwell on those matters."

"It's hard not to," I said.

"You won't be able to appreciate this for a long time, but I think you'll reach a higher place someday. I believe that."

Alisha looked at me, possibly trying to decide if I was open to whatever karmic trip she was about to lay at my feet. I remained neutral.

"When we suffer greatly and experience such loss and grief, we can achieve a greater understanding of humanity and loyalty and what it means to love."

"I guess."

"But we have to be open to it. And I think it takes a while to get there."

"Probably."

I inhaled her scent of fresh flowers and apricot while studying her face. Her skin was flawless. I guessed that I had at least seven or eight years on her. I was tempted to ask the source of her wisdom. I was tempted to ask if she was married. I was tempted to ask if she wanted to come home with me for the evening. Instead, I shook her hand and thanked her before heading out to the parking lot. Taking the long way home for once, I drove in silence through the dusky night, enjoying not only the peace, but the faint traces of Alisha's scent that clung to me with a sort of sad impermanence. When I got home, I celebrated the completion of my final session with a couple glasses of red wine and a good night's sleep.

•　　•　　•　　•　　•

During one of our first summer weekends together, Robbie and Riley and I shared a perfect Saturday. We spent hours at the beach, picnicking, visiting with friends, playing hide and seek and tag until we were all short of breath. It was dark by the time we got home and crawled into my bed to watch a movie. By 10:30, they had both given up the fight to stay up any later. Riley's eyes were getting dopey and Robbie had built his trademark blanket and sheet cocoon around his head, signifying he was ready to call it quits as well.

"Can we sleep with you, Daddy?" Riley asked.

This question was tantamount to "Are you okay with being kept up all night due to us tossing and turning and kicking and snoring?" But that night I said yes. I didn't care about losing sleep. I just needed the feeling from that day to last a little longer.

"Can you tell us a story?" Riley asked.

"Of course," I said, turning off the lights and TV.

No one mentioned how it had been a while since hearing one of my bedtime stories, how it was a tradition that had been abandoned back in January. Reveling in my chance for a comeback, I started talking. I didn't contemplate a plotline like I had often done in the past. Barely coming up for air, I told them a story about the Land of July, a strange and magical place that exists right here on earth. I described the strangeness and the magic to them in detail. There were long stretches of road made up of gleaming bright bouncy pads so you could leap miles into the air and all throughout the Land of July. There were trees that could be plucked from the ground and used to pole vault through the clear, open sky. At night, stars became edible and tasted like delicious rock candy. The sun, which was always cool enough to touch, had a spigot that produced icy cold lemonade.

There were heroes and villains in the Land of July. And I described these heroes and villains in detail. I told them about the enormous Fruit Fly Monsters who had slingshots strapped between their beady, bloodshot eyes and who would fire off putridly awful peaches and apples and pears at any good guy in their sights. I told them about the Geezers, grumpy old men who yelled and complained and detested fun and music, and with a swipe of their heavy steel canes could knock someone to the ground or crush their spirits. As for the heroes in the Land of July, there were two: a super-powered crime fighting duo who went by the name of R&R. In fact, it was due to R&R that the Land of July was so named, for it was their birth month. This fact alone made R&R a sort of King and Queen over the Land of July. And R&R's goodness meant their lives were guaranteed to be charmed no matter what kind of badness ever tried to take them down. After all, they were living in a place called the Land of July. And that meant so much. Everything, really.

From the faint glow of the nightlight, I could see that they were both smiling as they fought to stay awake. I paused for a moment to observe their amusement. When I did this, Riley spoke up, asking me a question in her sleepy little girl voice:

"Daddy, is the Land of July far from here?"

Sitting up in bed a little, I looked back and forth between both of their faces. The stillness of that single moment might as well have been staged. It was that perfect. My response, which I offered in a sort of dramatic hush, was meant to enchant and comfort my children before they fell asleep:

"Baby girl, the Land of July is so close that you just wouldn't even believe it. It really is. I promise."

As I drifted off to sleep that evening, I considered the summer months that lay ahead. The prospect of them rang in my brain like applause that went on for too long. Something was already tiresome about the season I had longed for these past many months. I could see its end already looming like some crooked detour sign that gave no alternate route. And I quickly remembered conversations I had with Robbie and Riley about the majesty of summer's potential, how it so soon vanishes, leaving us bitter and childlike in the new, darker light of autumn, and though we might be victims of its chicanery, we are still smitten with its resilience to return the following year and the following year and the following year.

My thoughts quickly turned to all that was imminent. Old age. Retirement. Death. Taxes. None of it mattered besides the one that did: the kids growing up and leaving me behind. Given the recent condition of my heart, this seemed less like a rite of passage and more like blasphemy. I went to bed that evening with the two saddest sentences echoing in my brain. *Now that summer's over. Now that the kids are grown.* Thank God I would never recall any dreams from that night, but it's easy to imagine they were full of frail and slight apparitions that could have spooked the absolute hell out of me.

Dear Bitterness,

I'm positive you've already decided that we'll be bound together for life. I imagine you've dug your foundation and burrowed yourself in good and deep, haven't you? You like it in there. I know you do. You like it where it's cool and dark and where you're mostly concealed from the outside world until you come out of hiding and dare the sunlight to burn a great wide hole through your fleshy belly. FYI, I've done a little research on Stockholm syndrome and have yet to make any clear determinations at this point. I tell you this only so you understand how seriously I am finally taking our alliance.

Don't be alarmed that I know you so well. And don't insult me by suggesting I don't. We both understand our relationship. The only thing I don't have a handle on is who courted who. Did I ring you up one desperate evening when I was eighteen or nineteen and searching for an identity and take you out and fling you into my life? Or did you pounce on me one night while I was drunk and lonely and spewing pseudo-intellect at girls in bars who might have liked the looks of me, but thought me pretty weird? Either way, we've been acquainted now for some time. And like a lot of relationships, especially the ones that don't need to exist, things have grown a bit stale. Especially during these past few years. Brace yourself, but here it goes: The sexy quotient has plummeted. You, my friend, are a super tight t-shirt, a backwards baseball cap, a convertible. And I am no longer twenty-years-old.

Please don't misunderstand me: This is not a fare thee well. Nor is it some delusional manifesto that I'm suddenly somehow a new man, a man who does yoga and lights candles and has a mantra and says things like "There but for the grace of God go I." I wouldn't insult you like that. Not to mention I have no room in my brain for such grandiose lies. But. Yes, there's a "but." But we must redefine our terms. Or, rather, I must. And I have. And here they are: You can stay put. I am not evicting you. Let's give you, say, squatter's rights. As for those redefined terms, they will be forthcoming and laid out by the two of us. A collaboration. I owe you that much, I suppose. So stick around if you must, but please know that you might start to feel cramped, claustrophobic even, once I send out some new invites I'm working on. Yes, I'm looking for some new company. Relax. This is a time consuming process. But it's imminent. So play nice and be respectful when it comes. Please. And if you do start thinking about opening up your old bag of tricks, just remember that I'm here to talk you down. But my patience, like those of everyone I love, are quite limited.

Respectfully,

Rob

Chapter 7

Allison's criminal case was a mystery to me. There were countless unanswered questions. What was the prosecution's angle? Were they using her taped confession I had turned over? What kind of deal was her attorney working on? Was she looking at doing real prison time? How was she funding it all?

I instigated no research into any of these matters. Of the many online links and stories my family sent me, I didn't read or watch a single one. Not the channel 8 coverage piece. Not the front page Hartford Courant article. Not the one in the New Haven Register. Not even her arrest warrant, which was made public. The contempt I had for her was put aside when I was faced with these assaults. The truth is that I felt protective of her when I saw that she was being portrayed like a criminal. There was a fleeting need to rescue her, defend her character, speak out against things that surely couldn't be true.

Then she would fuck with me and I'd root for her demise. Allison's transformation from desperate to ruthless dated back to January 30th when she was served with divorce papers and had me arrested the following day. Thus began her campaign to reduce me to the lowest possible terms so she could again consider us contemporaries. Some matters were trivial like the repeated texts she sent that threatened my job by telling me I was on my last legs at DHHS. Yet some made me want to feed her to the lions, like in the fall of 2015 when she dressed Robbie in a shirt two sizes too small for his first day of third grade.

The pinnacle of her erraticism was when she somehow managed to coerce our son into saying that I threw him into a wall. DCF was called and I was put under investigation.

"Have you lost your mind?" I exclaimed one morning while we

exchanged the kids in a Dunkin' Donuts parking lot.

"Not sure what you mean," she said, sticking her cell phone in my face and recording my every word.

This was a recent tactic of hers. Yet it was hardly a deterrent for me; if anything, it was a platform to denounce on film her many new transgressions about which I had just learned from my children. One involved their mother talking with them about Gabe and Zach. Another had her showing them images of September 11th. A particularly disturbing one was that she was openly discussing the suicide of our friend Amy.

"You're now lying to government agencies?" I said.

The kids were waiting in my car, listening to music and not privy to the conversation we were having. Allison, holding back the slightest trace of a grin, kept her phone steady, and just a few feet from my face.

"I'm worried," she said. "I'm worried about the kids."

"You're full of shit."

"Just let me take the kids and go."

"You're fucking crazy," I said, "do you know that?"

"I'm just worried about my children."

"You convinced our son to lie. Any idea how damaging that kind of manipulation is?"

I called her out on more of her nonsense, committing it all to tape. There was the rambling, hysterical voicemail she left on my phone just days earlier, pleading with me not to take the kids away from her, to put their needs above all else, to have mercy and compassion. The following day she called my father and stepmother, leaving them something of a different message, which proclaimed I was unstable and a threat to the kids. She even told Robbie and Riley to no longer come to me with their worries, but to instead run down the street to Mrs. Harmon's house.

With zero response to any of this, she kept her posture upright and that damn cell phone in my face. I sprang into full alpha mode, cursing and ranting and telling her again that she was ill and unstable. I finally took a deep breath and opened the car door; Robbie and Riley climbed out and went with their mother who I saw as being more desperate and dangerous than I ever had before. When I drove home, I emailed my attorney, telling him we needed to set up a meeting.

The following week we drew up a twenty-nine-point bulleted list that chronicled Allison's pernicious behavior. We even asked the court for copies of the text messages she sent her victims, feeling it might provide yet another window into her depravity. Our request was denied, shut down by her attorney who pointed out that this was evidence being used in an ongoing investigation. Feeling confident that we had enough material with our bulleted list, we filed a motion for an emergency change of custody on October 30th, 2015. I hand delivered the Ex parte to New Haven's Superior Court and awaited the judge's decision. It was granted within fifteen minutes. Walking out of the courthouse with the paperwork in my hand, I felt, for the first time in close to a year, relief, satisfaction, vindication. I wanted ten thousand more copies to sprinkle throughout the city streets. It was Friday, nearly 4:00, and not my scheduled weekend to be with the kids. So I had to race to the daycare to retrieve them, provide the owner with the Ex parte, and explain that the kids would be exclusively with me for the next two weeks until Allison and I battled it out in court. After I called my attorney to let him know the motion was granted, I phoned my mother:

"We got it," I said. "The judge granted it. We got it."

"That's wonderful!"

"Can you believe it? They're coming home."

"Where are the kids?"

"I'm going to pick them up right now."

"You must be thrilled."

"You have no idea."

The kids and I lived together, uninterrupted, for the next two weeks. Reunited under the same roof. I was able to see them every day after school and share meals with them each night. Robbie and I worked together on his fraction worksheets and Riley and I jumped on the trampoline in the backyard. The three of us played and watched movies and became a full time family again. Allison was ordered to keep her distance during that time. Other than by phone, there was a strict no contact rule. When the kids asked me why they were living with me seven days a week, I answered simply:

"Because this is your home."

"Are we going to see Mommy again?" they would ask.

"Of course you are."

"When?"

"We'll figure that out soon enough."

The court appearance was scheduled for November 13th. My attorney warned me it would be a bloody battle.

"She's got nothing to lose," he told me. "She'll go for broke. Your focus is to explain your concerns to the judge. Be direct and honest and specific."

"Any predictions?" I asked.

"None," he said. "It depends on how convincing you are that the children are in potential danger when they're with their mother."

"That shouldn't be difficult," I said. "We've compiled a hell of a list."

"The list is one thing," Ray pointed out, "*proving* what's on it is another."

Over the course of two separate two hour sessions at Ray's office, we went through a mock Q&A. His scrutiny was relentless. My response time was either too fast or too slow. My tone was too confident or too mopey. My body language, very important, needed to express assurance but not cockiness. And then there was the substance of my answers, which had to be solid. I was either too verbose or too vague. Don't use big words. Don't mumble. Don't lose your composure. Don't be defensive.

"Her attorney is going to hammer you," Ray explained. "And so is the judge."

No one knew the potential outcome. Yet we all understood that what hung in the balance was paramount. November 13th arrived. My mother and sister took the day off of work to join me and Ray and Hillary, Ray's paralegal, at the courthouse on 235 Church Street in downtown New Haven. When Allison arrived, wearing stockings, a skirt, and her hair in a tight bun, she was accompanied by her father and stepmother, who had made the drive all the way from Fredericton, New Brunswick to witness the high stakes standoff. Within minutes, Allison's attorney showed up. As a dead ringer for a balding, paunchy, middle aged Jiminy Cricket, he didn't look like much to me.

After some procedural logistics, we entered the courtroom. It was around 10:00 a.m. The judge was a serious looking, dark haired woman who appeared to be around sixty. We rose as she entered. She made some preliminary remarks and we were seated. Ray leaned towards me and told me I would be the first to take the stand. Then he whispered a quick reminder:

"Keep your answers short and factual and unemotional."

After being sworn in, I took a seat in the witness box, just a few feet from the judge. I was within the physical vantage point of challenging anyone in that courtroom to a staring contest. My mother. My sister. Allison. Her family. Her counsel. I asked the bailiff, a pleasant looking heavyset woman, for a glass of water. She politely refused. Ray began the questioning. He laid the foundation with inquiries about my name and age and residence and place of employment and the names and birthdays of Robbie and Riley. The first objection from Allison's attorney came when Ray asked me why I had filed for divorce back in January. The judge overruled it and we were off and running.

Ray, in a measured, matter-of-fact voice, asked me about Allison's behavior in the last few months. We discussed her boyfriend, Jeremy, and how my children had come to feel uncomfortable in his presence. We discussed the reports Robbie and Riley had given to me about talks they shared with their mother – talks about heady, confusing, inappropriate topics. We covered the voicemail messages and the DCF investigation. My voice, as I listened to it recall the events that had shaped my life, sounded like some foreign echo I would never again be able to describe to another breathing soul. My composure was intact. I was impassive and almost monotone. At one point, Ray asked me to speak up.

By the time Allison's attorney got to me, I was damp from perspiration and would have committed a crime for some water. I looked in the direction of my mother and my sister; they were still and expressionless.

"When did you begin having serious concerns about the welfare of your children, Mr. Marchese," her attorney asked.

"Many months ago."

"Many months ago?"

"Yes."

"Then why are we just now hearing about them?"

"Because I feel that her behavior has worsened as of late."

"Is that so?"

"Yes."

"And what about *your* behavior, Mr. Marchese?"

"What about it?"

"How would you describe it?"

"I'm not sure what you mean."

My answer seemed to beguile him. He turned his back to me and swiped a laptop from his briefcase.

"Your Honor," he said, "I'd like to play a recording for the court if I may."

The judge made no objections. She looked on with disinterest as the computer was plugged in and mic'd. I watched my mother and sister whisper to one another. Ray shuffled some papers, waiting to see what his opposition had planned. It occurred to me, probably seconds before it played, that it would be a recording of our Dunkin' Donuts exchange. It was. As she listened to the five-minute invective, the judge shook her head and rolled back her eyes.

"And with the children there the entire time," she said, looking at me once the tape stopped.

In a defeated voice, I replied that they were in the car with music blaring and couldn't have possibly heard the exchange. Allison's attorney was quick to rewind the last few seconds where the kids were climbing into their mother's car when I did happen to lunge one final insult while they were within earshot.

"Unbelievable," the judge said. "Just unbelievable."

A recess was called. I followed Ray and Hillary and my family into a small antechamber.

"That was fucking brutal," Ray said.

My mother wore a devastated expression.

"Did that tape just seal the deal?" I asked.

"Pretty much," Ray said.

"Are you kidding me?"

"The judge is pissed," he said. "There's only one translation there: She doesn't like you."

"So this comes down to a popularity contest?" I asked.

Hillary, a sweet, motherly type who sometimes had more compassion for my plight than my own family, was hopeful that the judge might still be shocked at Allison's bad behavior, which could possibly trump the tape.

"No way," Ray said. "If anything, she'll conclude that you're both out of your goddamn minds."

After the recess, things went from bad to worse. Allison took the stand and bawled like a woman who had been battered one too many times and was driven to desperate measures. It was a brilliant performance. Then, in a strange turn of events, my sister was called as a witness to help corroborate the chronology of some events discussed earlier. She not only faltered when the judge drilled her, but her testimony was ambiguous enough to appear as though we had conspired in a lie.

A second recess was called. Both attorneys met in the judge's chambers for nearly an hour. By the time Ray emerged, his face was a perfect expression of his earlier prediction. It took little time for him to lay out the terms:

"The judge thinks you're both full of shit. She has serious concerns about the kids being with either of you. She thinks you have nothing more than a chip on your shoulder and a vendetta against Allison. And she thinks Allison is just plain fucking crazy."

"So what now?" my mother asked.

"Supervised visits for both," Ray said. "You'll each need to be accompanied by approved chaperones when in the presence of your children. This will be for a period of a few weeks and then the judge will dissolve the marriage herself and we'll resume with the fifty-fifty custody arrangement."

I would have preferred to have my guts scraped out than adhere to this nonsense. Was this judge out of her mind? Was she even qualified to be making such decisions? Did she need to come to my house and witness firsthand how I cared for my children? Did she need to see our nightly dance parties? Or watch Riley get woken up each morning by Kirby the Tickle Spider? Or listen to Robbie hold entire conversations with Marjorie and Pearl, the two nutty senior citizens I would invoke in my best old lady voice?

"I need your list of chaperones," Ray said, handing me a pen and a piece of paper.

"This is bullshit," I said.

"No," he said, "this is the new deal. The alternative is to have the kids put in foster care."

The world had turned itself inside out. Logic and sanity and fairness were all rotting under the wormy soil. As far as the eye could see, there was nothing more than a swirling cesspool with vultures and villains hovering above, spewing gibberish I was forced to suck up into the back of my throat. And if I happened to choke on it, then so be it.

My mother moved in with me on the days I had the kids. Though she resigned to the arrangement, she was no doubt at her wit's end with her son's fuck-ups. My coping skills. My impulsivity. My refusal to see Jim the therapist on a regular basis. The damage was piling up. But she bailed me out. Again. And we made the best of it. The kids, who never once asked why their Mimi was living with us, loved having her stay the night and see them off to school in the morning. She cooked spaghetti and meatballs and watched me sulk around the house and throw my hands in the air in disbelief over the judge's decision. One night, when the dishes were done and the kids were in bed, she gave me an earful:

"I don't know why you think you're entitled to act like an asshole," she said. "You're not. No one is. What you say is often truthful, but how you say it is offensive and appalling. You're out of control and you're embarrassing yourself. Why can't you see that? Why can't you see that bad things happen to people all the time? But it's the moments of grace they exude in the aftermath that impresses people? All you seem to do is channel this wise-guy persona, which clearly does not, has not, and will not serve you well?"

The speech was an impassioned plea for me to get my head right. It was full of wisdom. My obligation to this woman who had borne my burdens like no one else, who had watched me make a pulpy mess out of already devastating circumstances, was to agree with her and apologize and tell her I would make an effort to fix myself. So I did just that. More out of deference than sincerity. The truth is that a meanness had grown inside of me. It had become natural for me to be a prick. There was no pretense about it. I was exorcising whatever was festering in my gut and my heart. I was being true to how I felt. Kindness. Mildness. Soft-spokenness. These were like casino coins I had been duped into surrendering to the house. Or maybe I gave them away in a foolish show of bravado. It hardly mattered. Either way, they were gone.

My relationship with Tosh ended the following week. It no longer suited my circumstances. The spirited party girl didn't deserve my fits of morose solitude.

"It's an act of mercy," I told her, "trust me."

"I don't want an act of mercy."

"I'm useless right now."

"So what?"

"I've got nothing to offer you."

"Not true."

"It *is* true. I'm King Midas in reverse."

"Then who's going to be your queen, Doll?"

This was no desperate girl. Her offer to see me through this new darkness was sincere. But I was firm. I didn't have the energy to put someone else through my ordeal. It would have made me beholden yet again. I couldn't afford this. My debts had already piled up beyond belief.

The single untainted element in my life became teaching, which had greatly improved since the previous school year. I left my misery at home and went to work each day without incident, talking Shakespeare and Thoreau with my students. It was during each of my classes that I felt the most normal, buoyed even. There was something about facing off each day with a room full of potential that restored me, at least for the time being. My students, always the best part of my job, could make me forget on certain days that I would be heading home to a house that now felt haunted to me.

As for my colleagues, I'm positive there were factions who wanted me gone. Some might have viewed me as a grotesque reminder of unthinkable events. They likely saw my presence as an act of defiance. Many sought me out during this new school year to ask how I was doing, to inquire about my children, to tell me to keep my head up. Those who called themselves my friends maintained their support and affection. Some ignored me altogether.

The English department, months away from finishing the curriculum we started the previous year, was sinking under deadlines, workshops, and the looming reality that the 2016–2017 school year would demand of us some very rigid expectations. Martha, who was leading this charge with Gail, the Assistant Superintendent, showed signs of constant struggle. Her curtness and condescension were elevated. Her impatience and favoritism manifested constantly. The district, recognizing how beleaguered Martha had become, even outsourced a woman named A.Z., who flew into Connecticut time and time again from Virginia Beach.

My relationship with Martha was tenuous at best. It had always been this way. She was often the loudest one in the room and I openly wore my disdain for such behavior. Yet we managed to move past our differences and work together amicably. This began to change in the fall of 2015 when it was revealed to me by my colleagues that she was disparaging me on a regular basis.

"She feels under the gun with this curriculum thing and needs a scapegoat," one of my peers pointed out. "And you're the Department Lead. That makes you an easy target."

My exchanges with Martha remained professional. Yet I could sense the stress she was feeling and I was careful to stay out of her way. Not to mention, she was as good as gone from Madison. The year before, she had announced that once the curriculum was written, she would be relocating down south, never to return to DHHS. She of course added to this declaration that working under me would be impossible for her ego.

On November 25th, the day before Thanksgiving, my relationship with Martha would reach a crucial impasse. The day was festive and spirited. Students and faculty were looking forward to a few days off. This would mark the first holiday I would spend without my children. All I had to look forward to was a meeting at Central Office that Gail had scheduled to discuss some matters with me and Martha. It was an hour to dismissal when one of my colleagues paid me a visit.

"I thought you might like to know about Martha's holiday plans," he told me.

"Why is that?"

"She's having Allison and the kids over."

This was like a random act of violence – a sudden slashing across the cheek with a straight edge razor. The truth is that Martha and Allison had hardly been friends at any point. It made no sense.

"You're kidding."

"Nope."

"That's fucked up."

"It *is* fucked up."

"I don't even know what to say."

"Just thought you'd want to know about it."

The truth is I didn't. It was useless information. Just another ugly moment to add to the mosaic.

The school day ended and I drove to Central Office. The three of us sat in a rear conference room and discussed an upcoming workshop we would be having with A.Z. My focus was consumed with how the very next day Martha would be sharing a holiday meal with Robbie and Riley. There was a brief lull in the meeting when Gail left the room for a moment. I seized the opportunity.

"Can I ask you something?" I said.

"What is it?" Martha said, avoiding eye contact.

"Are you having Allison and the kids over for Thanksgiving?"

"Yes."

That was all she offered. I'm not sure if it was the brevity or the flippancy of that single word, but either way I felt a brand new humiliation. And it was spit shined to perfection with Martha's saliva. Gail returned and the meeting resumed. It lasted another ten minutes or so. I said very little in that time. Quiet and mild mannered, I nodded and agreed with what was discussed. When it was over, we stood up and wished one another a happy holiday.

"Any special plans?" Gail asked.

"Not really," Martha said. "Just the usual."

Holding tight to myself, I took a long but quiet breath. Gail was looking in my direction. I forced myself to smile. Yet I struggled to speak. Shaking my head, I waited for the moment to pass before walking out ahead of Martha to the parking lot.

•   •   •   •   •

A few weeks later I was called down to my principal's office for an impromptu meeting. I walked into a rather daunting administrative triumvirate: T.J., Tom, and Gail. We shook hands and I took a seat at the head of the table.

"Thanks for meeting with us today," T.J. said. "And sorry to spring it on you last minute."

"No problem."

Tom and T.J. both turned to Gail, who wasted no time in leading the discussion.

"I wanted to meet with you today, Rob, to share some concerns I've been having and to see if we all might reach an understanding about where we're headed with our new curriculum."

I was intrigued.

"Absolutely," I said. "I'm all ears."

Gail told me she once saw me as having endless enthusiasms, which she described as infectious. My rapport with my colleagues, she said, was strong and vital. My ideas. My attitude. My leadership. She discussed all of these, delineating a *before* and *after.*

"I'm not sure what's changed," she said, "or if anything has in fact changed. But I need assurances that you feel ready to lead your department through some of the biggest advances it's ever seen."

Then she veered towards the specific. I was five minutes late to a sophomore curriculum workshop led by A.Z. a month or so ago. I left ten minutes early from another workshop, missing a debriefing session. There was the Thanksgiving Eve meeting where I seemed aloof and disinterested. All of what she said was true. Which is why I didn't become defensive. I apologized and declared my allegiance to the English Department and its initiatives.

"Wonderful," she said. "And please let me know if there's anything I can do to support you."

"Actually," I said. "There is."

It would have been too easy to sacrifice Martha at this moment. A cinch to announce that she was decimating the curriculum project. Child's play to point out how she was not only abrasive towards everyone in her path, but that she lacked any ability to lead, collaborate, communicate, and, most importantly, inspire. I could have stated that nothing whatsoever was clear in the way of deadlines or expectations or even consequences for not piloting certain lessons and units of study. It would have been easy to illuminate any of these points by reminding Gail that the district was shelling out thousands of dollars to A.Z. who had been hired to more or less do Martha's job for her. Instead, I asked if there might be a way to streamline and organize our agenda. Maybe create a calendar, something to allay the confusion, something tangible to look at so we all understood what was expected of us.

"Maybe a spreadsheet," Gail offered.

"That'd be great."

"Perfect."

A couple of things happened at the end of that school day. The first one is that T.J. called me down to his office to slap me on the back and tell me how well I handled myself in our meeting and how the points I brought up were all valid. The second one is that Gail, who somehow found the time that afternoon, sent the department a meticulous spreadsheet that delineated everything we had discussed. I thought well of both these gestures. Yet my mind was more consumed with considering just how much scrutiny I seemed to be under.

•   •   •   •   •

On December 1st, the bogus DCF claim against me went unsubstantiated. Robbie was interviewed and confirmed that I never laid a hand on him. Three days later, on Friday, December 4th, the divorce was finalized. As turbulent and drawn out as it had been, I made out well. My only obligation, aside from the lump sum of cash I had to pay my ex-wife, was that I would be responsible for all expenditures pertaining to my children. I took this on with nothing but pride. The house was now in my name and I was financially free and clear. The most important facet turned out to be that I would not be mandated to have Robbie and Riley visit their mother should she be incarcerated.

I found myself mostly inactive that day. I spoke very little and did next to nothing. I tried to read, but had trouble focusing. I skimmed Netflix, but couldn't find anything worth watching. My mother was no longer required to stay with me; this didn't stop her from calling that evening to urge me to keep my mind occupied. A few texts came in congratulating me on being single. Out of politeness, I responded with a "Thank you" each time. One text came from a coworker who never dropped Allison as a Facebook friend. It was a screenshot of a recent selfie Allison had taken, preening for the camera, her hair bleached blonde and her lips pursed. The posting beneath the picture read "Getting divorced sucks – being divorced doesn't."

My final meeting with Jim the therapist occurred a few days later. We never quite connected. The truth is I was hardly an ideal patient. I would make appointments, then cancel the day before. Or I would take weeks off in between visits.

"I think I need to recommend another therapist," he told me in the middle of our session.

"Really?"

"I feel that my schedule is too busy."

"And you've just now realized this?"

"Yes."

"*Just now?* In the middle of our hour together?"

"I feel that your problems might be better suited for another therapist."

"Is it that your schedule is too busy or is it that my problems are too burdensome?"

"It's both."

"Is this even ethical to do?"

"I think it would be best to go our separate ways."

On my way out the door, he reminded me to mail him his thirty-dollar copay.

"Of course," I said. "Your money. Absolutely."

I called my mother from the parking lot.

"He fired me," I told her, laughing heartily. "Jim the goddamn therapist just fired me."

She found the humor as well and we laughed together. Yet her voice sobered instantly when she made me promise to waste no time in finding a new therapist.

I filled out and mailed the check the minute I arrived home. On the bottom portion, to the left of where I sign my name, my checks have the word "For" and then a blank space. I wrote, in small, lowercase letters, "nothing."

Amidst all of these endings came something wonderful and unexpected. I met and fell in love with H.B.B., a tall, wild-haired girl who proved my equal in countless ways. She could be a smartass one minute and solitary the next. She was sensitive and dog obsessed and snorted when she laughed and had no problem telling me I was being a prick when I misbehaved. She loved old Woody Allen and Hitchcock films and she owned a record player and a fine collection of Grateful Dead and Marshall Tucker Band albums.

I took my time in introducing her to Robbie and Riley. When I did, the three of them got along like long lost friends. They teased each other and played Hungry Hungry Hippos and the four of us shared meals together and watched *The Wonder Years*. She eventually met the rest of my family who took to her right away. When I asked myself if I could see this tall, wild-haired girl in my future with me and Robbie and Riley, the answer was always the same, and always made me smile in spite of myself. It even coaxed a new song out of me that hardly hid behind abstraction.

"Hallelujah Girl"

Hallelujah girl, I've been dying to sing this song / Dying to sing this song
I've been waiting with pride by the riverside for you to come along
Hallelujah girl, you've been making me believe / Making me believe
You've got the hands of a healer and a blackjack dealer – You're bringing me to my knees

Hallelujah girl, hallelujah girl, hall-e-lu-jah

Hallelujah girl, I'm starting to see the light / Starting to see the light
You cured my blindness with love and kindness and stayed with me all night
Hallelujah girl, you fill me up with praise / Fill me up with praise
It ain't hard to tell you're no Jezebel – You got sins like summer days

Hallelujah girl, hallelujah girl, hall-e-lu-jah

Hallelujah girl, I'm dreaming of tent revivals / Dreaming of tent revivals
Singing sweet and so complete, singing for my survival
Hallelujah girl, I'm calling your name out loud / Calling your name out loud
Like a Sunday prayer, it's in the air, ringing pure and proud

Hallelujah girl, hallelujah girl, hall-e-u-jah

With tongue-in-cheek lyrics, the song was nevertheless a mini celebration that I had been renewed. My voice had risen, ever so slightly, and my eyes had brightened a bit. Embracing the future once again became viable. Yet this did little to allay the burdens hefted on me by my ex-wife, who had become an endless source of intrigue to me as I watched her life from afar. Friends would share with me Allison's countless selfies, close-up glamour shots that belied her lot, or inspirational quotes she would promulgate from sources like Maya Angelou and Buddha. I began asking myself who this person was and if I had ever really known her in all the years we had been together. I began reading about narcissism and borderline personality disorder. My research yielded more than a few a-ha moments. Yet I recognized this as an answerless quandary. Nothing could satisfy my curiosity. There was a part of me that longed to talk with her, to part through the wreckage that had become her reality and have an almost intervention-like heart-to-heart so I might learn something about the madness that had consumed her. There was another part of me that wanted her to simply disappear forever.

On February 12th, 2016, after playing at Donovan's Reef, a bar in downtown Branford, I drove to Allison's apartment, a colossal white multi-family house on East Main Street. She lived in apartment #2 on the second floor. Parking my car down a dead-end side street, I walked the short distance to the property and stood in the driveway, staring up at the house. It was close to 2:00 a.m. The sky was lit with a bright half-moon and the night was still. With my eyes fixed on the home's second story windows, I became suddenly aware of how divided my thoughts were. Some were full of bittersweet wonder over where my two young children were sleeping and how they ended up in such a foreign place. Others were full of savagery. It felt like I should have been holding my head in my hands so it wouldn't detonate right then and there. After circling the front lawn a few times, I forced myself from the ether of my aimlessness and walked back to my car. Driving home that night, I began to consider what I might actually be capable of doing. It didn't feel like a game to me, either. It felt as real and as harrowing as solitude does at 2:00 a.m.

Dear Past,

You are endlessly fascinating to me. This is not meant as flattery. Just an observation. You might very well be the single most potent intangible force ever known to humankind. Sounds dramatic, but I believe it to be true. How you manage to have existed, past tense, and somehow still exist, is one hell of a trick. You're a mirage and a brick wall within the same millisecond. You can turn people into dreamers or demons in the blink of an eye. You can cause tidal waves or absolute inertia. You scare, taunt, tempt, inspire, inform, motivate, masquerade, confuse, and consume with more gravitas than I can comprehend.

You're a legend. And your ego must be epic. Again, this is not meant as flattery. I'm just trying to lay it all out there so we can move forward. But I suppose moving forward is like kryptonite to you. I suppose there really is no moving forward with you. I recognize what I'm up against where you're concerned. I've never misjudged or underestimated you for a minute. If anything, I've fixated on you to the point where I could describe you to a sketch artist and they might render scrolls worth of picture perfect images that would be as lifelike as one of those Pedro Campos paintings.

I don't have a plan to bound and gag you and stick you in a crawl space where I'll visit on occasion and arrogantly demand that you've feasted long enough on my sanity and therefore finally got what you deserve and must live out your days without sunlight or sustenance. The truth is that I have no plan whatsoever. I'm well aware of what you are and where you stand and how what you illuminate is as blinding to me as a trillion constellations.

We are wedded to one another. This is true. Till death do us part. All that shit. I get it. I don't have options here. Memories are immutable – Eternal Sunshine of the Spotless Mind was only a film. I refuse to insult you by staging some sort of duel between the two of us. I won't embarrass myself in this way. This letter then really serves little to no purpose, other than to say that I'll be seeing you. As if you didn't know that already.

Respectfully,
Rob

Chapter 8

On February 26th 2016, the Hartford Courant ran a front page story on Allison entitled "Madison Teacher Pleads Not Guilty to Sexual Assault Charges." It was a follow up to one of her recent court appearances. My mother called me to discuss it.

"It's pretty brutal," she said. "Did you read it?"

I told her I did not, nor did I plan to. She told me that the reporter had devoted the last paragraph to me. In a single sentence, it conveyed that I was a teacher in Madison, that I had been arrested back in January of 2015, and was granted entry into the family violence program.

"They just can't leave you alone," my mother said.

"I guess not."

Then she pointed out something I hadn't quite considered:

"This has to infuriate the school's administration. They're just looking for this thing to go away. Fat chance."

I pictured a secret Central Office meeting between Tom and T.J. and Gail. One of them would toss the article onto Tom's desk and declare the magnitude of the problem that just wouldn't quit. They would talk about damage control one minute and letting the thing play itself out the next. A few tenuous solutions would be suggested and dismissed just as quickly. Someone would ask if the board of ed. had anything to offer on the matter. And then, presented not so much as an afterthought, but more as the true nature of their dilemma, the most tangible piece perhaps, someone would bring up Rob Marchese. This would cause them all to exhale deeply and shrug their shoulders, as if to say, "We'll see."

•   •   •   •   •

On March 4th, my band was playing at Asti in Branford when one of my friends and coworkers showed up a few minutes before we went on. She and I had much in common. Leading the list was our intolerance for Martha.

"I've got some news for you," she told me while I was tuning up. "Martha claims that the superintendent is urging her to apply for the English Coordinator job."

The position, which I was currently holding, was up at the year's end, and was open to anyone who had the proper certification. This meant Martha and myself. Having already applied, I had an interview scheduled for March 22nd.

"She made it seem like she had Tom's own personal endorsement. She's ridiculous."

"I thought she was moving down south," I said.

"So did I. So did *everybody.*"

"Well, I'm still hopeful," I said. "I've got to be."

Three days later, I was summoned to the principal's office. When I arrived, T.J. asked me to close the door and take a seat. One of the Assistant Principal's was in on the meeting.

"We've got a situation," T.J. said.

The early morning sunlight was blinding me through his office window. I shielded my vision as he spoke.

"We've just been notified that Allison has been texting with one of your students," he said.

Closing my eyes, I began to rub the sockets with the tips of my fingers. The Madison Police soon arrived and joined the discussion. T.J. continued. Not only was Allison reaching out to one of my students, but she was inquiring about Gabe, who had since left the district to enroll in private school.

"I wanted you to hear this from us," he said. "That's why I called you down."

The police talked a bit on the matter, telling me both boy's parents would be notified, as well as the prosecution in Allison's criminal case.

"Naturally," I said.

"We can't have you discussing this with *anyone*," T.J. said. "Especially your student. Do you feel you can do this?"

"Yes."

"Can I send you back to class, or do you need to take a break?"

"I'm good," I said, "I won't say anything."

"Are you sure?"

"I'm sure."

My head throbbed for the rest of the day, which saw me speak little and teach even less. That night I took an Ambien at around 8:00 and slept like the dead.

●   ●   ●   ●   ●

March 22nd arrived. It was my understanding that my interview would take fifteen minutes and would be conducted by five members of my department as well as the principal himself. When I met with T.J. in the main office at a few minutes before 2:30, he explained to me that there was a change in plans.

"The committee's going to be larger than intended," he said, leading me towards the conference room. "More than three times the size to be exact. Just wanted you to know. We'll each ask you one question, give you a chance to address questions of your own, and have you on your way. Sound good?"

"Sure."

There was no time to ask why the original plan had changed. So I followed my boss into the conference room, feeling quite certain that my paranoia, though not fully formed at that point, was justified. It's true that I was greeted with a sea of smiling faces that were all familiar to me. It's true that some were even my good friends, and all were colleagues I respected and admired. Yet I was still stuck by the notion that no one assembles a committee of seventeen at the last minute.

Coordinators from most departments were there. Members of guidance. Both Assistant Principals. Seven or so members of my own department, minus Martha, and Aim, the woman who loves anagrams.

It took less than half an hour for the committee to ask their questions and consider my responses. I felt positive about what I had to say. The truth is that for two years I had been doing the very job for which I was interviewing. Thanking them all for their time, I stood up and wished them a pleasant afternoon. T.J. told me he would be in touch. He was. That same evening, in fact. When I checked my work email three hours later, I found one telling me that there were some recent allegations against me that had been serious enough to put me under investigation. I was told to meet with him, Heather from Human Resources, and the superintendent the following morning. It was my right, the email stated, to bring with me union representation. It's likely that I read the thing at least twenty times. Then I spent the next few hours going over in my mind possible misdeeds I might have committed.

There was the recent Hemingway story, "The Killers," that I had taught to my American Lit. classes. The story uses the "n" word a number of times, but I had taken white out to each of them and inserted the word "bleep" in their place. I had shown my sophomores, who had just finished *Night* by Elie Wiesel, the Polanski film, *The Pianist*. But I had each student bring home a permission slip that explained the appropriateness and relevance of the Holocaust film. As a journal prompt, I showed my Creative Writing class a clip from episode six in season two of FX's *Louie*. The clip shows Louie confronted with two very disparate walks of life on a NYC subway platform: one, a virtuosic busker playing gorgeous violin music, and the other an obese homeless man who lays out a tarp over which to bathe his filthy body with a bottle of water.

I was at a loss. Nothing I had done seemed serious enough to warrant an investigation. I took another Ambien that night. It did nothing.

The meeting was scheduled for 9:30 a.m. It was held in T.J.'s office. I refused my right to have a union rep present. Seated once again at the head of the table, we got down to it. A formal by-the-book introduction was given by T.J. - something like "We are here to discuss recent grievances against you that have been brought to our attention; we will review them with you, ask you some questions, and then give you an opportunity to tell us anything that might help in our investigation." Heather, the HR woman, with her dark eyes and deadpan glare, began by telling me there were accusations that I had disparaged my ex-wife in a department meeting the previous school year, that I had spoken explicitly about sex acts she had committed with one of her victims, that I had made colleagues uncomfortable by doing so. Further allegations had me commenting on the attractiveness of a female candidate we interviewed the previous spring. I was said to have also talked about members of the staff I thought were sexy. Finally, an accusation stated that I used threatening language as well as my supervisory role to declare that I was in charge and certain individuals were beneath me, that I was the boss, and was therefore the one with the power and control.

The breakneck pace of these charges scrambled my thinking. I felt like I was dumping buckets of water from a sinking ship in order to stay afloat. When Heather came up for air, my brain succeeded in what I thought to be a miracle, especially given the stressfulness of listening to her. It was able to not only consider a single question – Where in god's name are these absurd allegations coming from? – but it was able to answer it as well: Aim, the woman who loves anagrams.

This was a private thought. It was nothing I could voice – at first anyway. I had to be careful how I responded. Identifying the culprit would be seen as an admission of guilt on my part. The truth is that Aim and I *had* discussed Allison the previous winter when I paid a visit to her classroom. But that was a private conversation – the one and only private conversation Aim and I had in a year and a half. The thought of me discussing such matters in a department meeting was laughable. The parts about praising female candidates or talking about female staff wasn't even steeped in a version of the truth. Lies. Plain and simple. As was the part about claiming myself to be the boss, the one in charge with power and control. With all the temperance I could muster, I denied these charges while looking into the eyes of everyone in the room. There was a lull for a few moments while notes were taken on laptops.

Then it was T.J.'s turn. There was an allegation that I cancelled department meetings at the last minute. Or didn't hold meetings at all when I was supposed to. That I went out of my way to exclude members of the department from email chains. That I sent one particular email to the department with the title "Earn a free massage from a homeless man." That I left a March 15th curriculum workshop a half hour early. Many complaints in this batch, I surmised, had come from Martha. She was hardcore when it came to meetings, especially since she had usurped most of them for her precious curriculum.

I was given a chance to respond. The only meetings I ever cancelled were ones I had *permission* to cancel. Permission I had gotten from T.J. The only occasions I ever left people off emails were when I would send something pertinent to just *freshman* teachers, or just *senior elective* teachers. As far as the homeless man quip, yes, that was true – just some absurd levity meant to amuse and entice people to open their email.

After more notes were taken, I was asked if there was anyone they should speak with who might be helpful in this investigation.

"Yes," I said, "anyone in the English department who is not Martha or Aim, the woman who loves anagrams."

"Anything else you'd like to add?"

"Just that the timing of this seems very interesting to me – the day after my interview. It's obvious who these complaints are coming from: two people who are sympathetic with my ex-wife. Not to mention, so many of these complaints are a year and half old. Isn't there a statute of limitations on filing a complaint against a coworker?"

They responded to not one of these points.

"There's one more thing," T.J. added. "You are not to discuss this matter with any of your colleagues. This is an active investigation and it must remain confidential while it's being carried out. Do you understand this?"

"I do."

The meeting was over. They told me they would be in touch. I thanked them for their time and headed up to the third floor. As I walked through the halls, my head bowed more than usual, I avoided eye contact with passersby. I was fixated on each step I took on the gleaming industrial vinyl flooring that the custodians always kept so immaculate. There was a sense of relief that I was headed back to the comfort of my students and books in room 338. There was an equal sense of dread each time my feet hit the ground; as fantastical as it sounds, I believe I feared the floor would turn to quicksand that would swallow me whole before I ever made it back safely to my classroom.

•   •   •   •   •

Focusing on anything other than the investigation became impossible. My appetite was obliterated. Sleep was erratic. With reluctance, I told my family about what was happening. They pointed out what anyone with plain vision could see: that the absurdity far outweighed the severity.

"Are they kidding?" my father asked. "They're bringing up issues that might have happened over a year ago?"

"This is very transparent," my stepmother said. "They will see that. Robbie and Riley could see that. I don't believe in coincidences. This is happening now for a reason. Because there are people who don't want you to get that job. Just see how it plays out. Be patient and see how it plays out."

"I wonder if Allison lent a hand in this thing," I said.

My father and Helene didn't hesitate to confirm that this was a vital possibility. The three of us marveled over the carelessness of my ex-wife toying with my job.

"It hurts your kids more than anyone," Helene said. "But then again, her thoughts have never once had their best interests at heart. Look at what she's done to your family."

My sister and mother provided equal solace. They saw the obviousness of the matter. The timing of the allegations being the day I was interviewed. The complaints all coming from Martha, and Aim, the woman who loves anagrams.

"Be patient," my sister said. "It'll be fine."

Patience was difficult to come by. The waiting was brutal. I wanted to prove my innocence. Enlisting a member of the tech department to assist me, I located every email I sent my colleagues from August to March. Printing off each one, I bound and labeled them and turned them into T.J. I also printed off an email Martha had sent that listed a dozen or so scheduled department meeting dates that she usurped for her own purposes. I even printed the March 15th page from my Outlook calendar, which specified that the day's workshop ended at 3:00, which is when I left. Finally, I put a call in to my doctor's office, who sent me a letter confirming my January 13th physical, which was the day I left the workshop ten minutes early.

T.J. took the bundle of papers from me with a roll of the eyes, adding that it would take hours for him to sort through.

"I get that," I said. "But I'm trying to prove I've got nothing to hide."

"I understand."

"There's not one moment that occurred this school year or last, in a meeting or an email or a private conversation, where I was unprofessional," I said. "So I titled an email with a ridiculous heading. So what. It's not lurid or sexual. This is all some sort of vendetta. And I'll do whatever I need to do to prove that I've done nothing wrong."

That was the extent of my dramatic speech. It was simply stated and even keeled. Yet it didn't move him in the least. Putting the papers on his desk, he told me to have a nice afternoon.

The days were piling up on top of one another. My peers constantly asked me about the Coordinator position and if I had heard anything. I told them I was positive I would not be receiving good news. The majority of them most likely knew about the investigation. I imagined them being pulled into T.J.'s office, one by one, and asked a litany of questions about my character, my leadership, my work ethic. I was unfazed by any answers they might give. Yet my anxiety and adrenaline were out of control; I could feel them inside my body, toxic, bubbly chemicals violently swirling in a black pool.

Within a few days, I received an email from T.J. I later learned that a facsimile was sent to Martha. They were sent in the morning, followed shortly by another one to the entire English department:

Email #1:

Good afternoon Rob,

Thank you for your interest in the English Program Coordinator vacancy. I apologize that it has taken me some time to inform you of your status but I take hiring very seriously. After reviewing a variety of factors, I regret to inform you that I will not be recommending you for this position. I understand this is not the outcome you were hoping for.

As discussed in the interview, you will still be an important member of the English department.

I look forward to our continued work at Hand.

Email #2:

Good afternoon,

I am sending this email as an update regarding the hiring process for the English program Coordinator vacancy. I have spent a great deal of time considering a variety of factors before making this difficult decision. At this time, I plan to move forward with posting this vacancy externally. Based on the submitted applications, I will create a hiring process that I will share with you in the near future.

For your information, the internal candidates have been informed of their status. Additionally, the current faculty member who will be the subject of a Reduction in Force as a result of this decision has been made aware of this information.

Let me know if you have any questions.

Colleagues stopped me in the hall that day to offer their sympathies. Many confided that they were relieved that at least Martha didn't get the job. Even the "reduction in force," a new teacher whose dismissal at the end of the school year was just made public, was supportive. As for Martha, I was told she threw a fit at her downtown office, cursing, crying, even hurling a book against the wall.

My own catharsis turned out to be a bit more damaging. Operating on impulse, I began talking about the ongoing investigation. Seeking out a few colleagues, I asked questions about my behaviors: Did I in fact disparage my ex-wife? Did I act inappropriately? Did I randomly cancel meetings? With no ill intent in making these inquiries, I told myself I wasn't doing anything wrong. I was merely trying to glean information from a period in time through which I might have been in some sort of fugue state. Besides, I decided, my colleagues – save Martha and Aim, the woman who loves anagrams – certainly had my back; they would never betray me – especially after all I had been through. Their reactions supported this: pleasant smiles accompanied by mild affirmations that I had been doing a fine job.

March 31st. It was a Thursday. At 11:00, I was in the middle of teaching *The Great Gatsby* to my Honors American Lit. class when I was given coverage before being summoned to T.J.'s office. I was greeted by the same threesome as before. They asked if I wanted a union rep. I accepted. T.J. did all the talking. He asked if I recalled our March 23rd meeting when I was told to not discuss the investigation. I nodded. He informed me that it was brought to his attention that I had in fact been discussing it. No questions were asked of me. Instead, instructions were given: head back to my room, which would be empty, as my students had been relocated, gather my belongings, speak to no one, leave the building immediately. I would be placed on paid administrative leave. The conditions were that I was to not set foot on school grounds. I was not to email anyone at the school or speak with students or employees. The administration would be in touch to let me know the next step.

The drive home was strangely peaceful. There were barely any other cars on the road. The weather was pleasant that day. Mild and mostly sunny. There was nothing to distract me from what had just happened. There was no indication of what *would* happen. Yet there was something enjoyable about the act of driving. I'm not sure if it was the control I had, or the flight I was achieving. Either way, I had a sudden fantasy about picking up Robbie and Riley from school, stopping home to pack a few things, then pointing the car in whatever direction my impulses dictated. Obviously I did not do this. For a number of reasons. The main one being that my impulses no longer seemed to be all that reliable.

·   ·   ·   ·   ·

April of 2016 was a busy month – despite me not going to work every day. On the 1st, I saw my doctor who prescribed Alprazolam, which is an anti-anxiety med. A wonderful little pill, it's likely something I should have been on since January of 2015. It not only helped me sleep, but it managed to remove my heartbeat from my throat and restore it to my chest. That same day, Allison texted my family to let them know that she was predicting a complete breakdown on my part. She demanded that they encourage me to get professional help or else she would pursue legal measures to take the kids from me. This seemed to confirm that she was being fed information by Martha and Aim, the woman who loves anagrams. If I needed further proof of this, I received several texts of my own from Allison, stating how she had received numerous calls and emails from my former coworkers alerting her that I had lost my job.

On April 2nd, an article was published in the New Haven Register on teacher/student sex scandals. It was of course another expose on Allison and her ongoing case. On April 4th, channel 8 picked up the story and ran an exclusive on same thing. This time, the superintendent himself was interviewed. The name "Marchese" must have woken him up at night. It must have rung in his ears like some black magic curse. In the meantime, I was receiving constant texts from my ex-wife. She asked me if I was moving, selling the house, looking for another job. I didn't respond to any of it.

My family intervened. They had chalked up some practice in dealing with my calamities, so they were better prepared this time. I received lectures and tough love and hopeful wishes and practical, obvious bits of wisdom.

"This is not a done deal," my sister told me. "It's likely that this will get you a slap on the wrist, but I'm sure you're not going to lose your job over it."

If anyone was an authority on this type of matter, it was my sister. As a Central Office administrator herself, Amy knows the process pertaining to reprimands.

"They will see this as insubordinate," she said, "but given the circumstances, I cannot imagine it's a fireable offense."

My father and stepmother, also public school administrators, cast aside pragmatics and looked at the human element.

"These fucking people," my father said. "These *mother*fucking people. Don't they know there's a family at stake here? A family with two small kids. My grandchildren. Those *mother*fuckers."

The motherfuckers, in my mind, encompassed a litany of individuals: Martha, Aim, the woman who loves anagrams, Allison, T.J., Tom. Anyone who had either set out to destroy me or lacked the compassion to forgive my idiocy.

"So you talked," my father said. "Jesus Christ, who wouldn't? The position they put you in. The worry and the anxiety, day in and day out."

He became my spokesman. This gave me a slight reprieve. All I had to do was nod my head and shrug my shoulders when he came to my defense.

"Did they think they were investigating a triple homicide?" he said. "Self-important pricks."

If my mother heard this, she would have doubled over in disgust. She subscribed to a much more rigorous, rule-following standard of living. Not that my old man was a renegade, or a proponent of flouting convention. He was not. Is not. Yet his true education, he would say, was from the streets. And it dictated loyalty, mercy, common sense.

"You continue to do this to yourself," my mother told me. "It's getting tiresome. You truly are your own worst enemy. Why can't you see this?"

"I *can* see it."

"Then why can't you control it?"

"I don't know."

174

"You managed to have a nice run for a few months. And now this."

"I know."

"Your circumstances are certainly unique," she pointed out. "It's fairly obvious that there were some people behind the scenes who helped bring this on. But still."

My family made a lot of phone calls on my behalf. To HR people, superintendents, principals, anyone in the know on matters such as mine. They all learned the details of my case and each one predicted a positive outcome for me. They all saw me returning to DHHS, yet each one asked the same question: "Why on earth would I *want* to?"

"We have to hope there's enough good faith between you and your bosses for them to look past this," my mother said. "We'll see."

She again pointed out her deep concern over the recent media exposure on Allison's scandal. The timing of these pieces couldn't have been worse for my dilemma, not to mention my name in the district. Depending on how one viewed the situation, I had finally given just cause to once and for all do away with this blasted Marchese family.

A union rep from the Connecticut Education Association named Tom was assigned my case. We spoke on the phone long enough for me to tell him all that had gone down the past two school years. A meeting was scheduled at his Waterbury office for April 14th. My sister asked if she could attend.

Whatever hard won victories I had achieved since January of 2015 were gone. I was back in the land of panic and doubt. This time I had myself to blame. If only I had seen a therapist earlier. If only I had kept my mouth shut during the investigation. If only I could have remained focused more on progress rather than the past.

I lost twelve pounds in two weeks. I didn't play a note of music with my friends. I barely left the house. I gave one hell of a scare to that tall, wild-haired girl who brought me food and movies while I either rambled on about my life being over or said nothing at all. And Robbie and Riley. I'd like to say I did well at faking it for them, that I put on a convincing facade, one hell of a performance. But they had to have sensed my malaise. I cared for their basic needs, but couldn't seem to go above and beyond. Silliness subsided. Creativity was deferred. Each time

I saw their faces or heard their voices, I was reminded of my failures. They didn't deserve me and their mother. We had let them down. This was an understatement. We had taken their childhood, which is nothing less than a sacred promise, guarded over and blessed by hopeful intentions, and graffitied it with our grimy adult fuck-ups.

Since I felt like a loser, I figured I'd write a song that immortalized my collapse. So I combined my self-defeatism with my need to run away, even sneaking in a line for my tall, wild-haired girl, who was obsessed with having lived down south for a number of years. I named the song "As Far as Losers Go."

I hurl my silence into space / And drag my heartache all over the place
I count my angels before they resign / And watch them add up to ninety-nine
You're a southern girl, not born and bred / *Eat a Peach* is playing in your head
You're hard on me / Like a drunken dream / You're the finest martyr I've ever seen

We're restless, darling / And it shows / As we run from Cheyenne to New Mexico
Tripping over what overflows / And landing as far as losers go / Landing as far as losers go

You're honeysuckle, so fierce and twisted / And I'm holdin' on like you insisted
I'm burning up like an effigy / Should I feel flattered you sacrificed me?
I'm a washed up artist without a metaphor / You're a hardened killer without a killing floor
I'm bold as hell, like a prison break / You're hard to hold and harder to take

We're restless, darling / And it shows / As we run from Cheyenne to New Mexico
Tripping over what overflows / And landing as far as losers go / Landing as far as losers go

My April 14th meeting was as integral as it was useless. CEA Tom, a kind, soft-spoken man in his fifties, insisted on once again learning every detail that shaped my professional life in the last year and a half. So with my sister by my side, I started from the beginning, which was January 7, 2015. I told him about Allison's crimes and their impact on my job. I talked about my own arrest. About Martha and Aim, the woman who loves anagrams. I talked about my recent interview and the investigation and how everything had turned to shit in a matter of days. I provided him with relevant texts and emails and doctor's notes.

Tom listened, scribbling furiously on a yellow legal pad. He was unemotional about my story. He had a job to do and it ended there. I was looking for outrage and maybe even a little pity. A very real fantasy lived inside my head. And it had Tom exploding with disbelief over how I had been treated.

"This thing reeks of a conspiracy," CEA Tom would have said in my hypothetical world. "Anyone can see that. You've had impossible circumstances to deal with, not to mention despicable individuals colluding with your ex-wife. We're going to point out all of this and get you back in that building. It'll be as easy as that."

The reality is that his role was to make sure my interests were represented. In my mind, this translated to little more than being seated next to me at some future meeting where I would be read the riot act before summarily losing the job I had worked at for the past twelve years.

"There's no telling what will happen," he said. "They have you on insubordination. That's enough to get rid of you right there."

"So that's it?"

"Not necessarily," he said. "There *are* a number of other factors at play. There's the relationship between your ex-wife and some of these coworkers of yours. Not to mention your recent commitment to getting professional help. Our hope is that they'll account for these factors."

We would find out on April 20th. A 10:00 a.m. meeting was scheduled with the usual three, plus the school board's attorney from

Shipman & Goodwin. It was to take place in T.J.'s office at DHHS. This made me hopeful. At least they didn't shudder at the idea of me re-entering the building. The night prior to the meeting, while I was going over in my head the questions I might be asked, CEA Tom called to tell me the location had been moved to Central Office.

"Just answer their questions," CEA Tom told me the following day. "Don't offer more than what's necessary. If we need to take five, we'll take five."

Also joining us while we waited in the Hammonasset Room was Steve, the union rep from DHHS. I thanked him for his appearance as the interested parties entered. It was the usual group: Heather from HR, T.J., and Tom, the superintendent. This time they were joined by the district's lawyer, who looked like he stepped from the pages of a John Grisham novel. His gray hair was combed back in immaculate strokes and his suit was pressed and flawless. Hands were shaken and tables rearranged to face off with one another – me and my pathetic team on one side and those who controlled everything and had all the power and answers and authority on the other.

Dear DHHS Students,

I have listened to your complaints through the years and I'd say I've understood them well. Too much work. Too little free time. Too many expectations. Curfews. Rules. Parents. I get it. Much of it has boiled down to a rather sophomoric grievance of yours: It's not fair. Feel free to embrace this platitude and take it with you into adulthood where you should count on still finding a use for it.

There are far too many memories and faces to pour over in what will be a short letter. Please know that I can get sentimental with little effort. Yet I will do my best to keep away from such an atrocity. I'm not romanticizing our alliance, either. The truth is that it suited me like nothing I could have imagined. What a run. Twelve years. That comes out to about a thousand of you. I accept how the exchange works: I was forgettable to some, while some were forgettable to me. That's fine. But I never had a single doubt that I chose the right profession and discipline and town and school.

It became common for some of you through the years to ask me why I chose to do what I do. My answer never varied. "Because adults suck," I would say. "And I'd rather be unemployed than work with them." Maybe I was being dramatic, but that's not too far from my position. Who knew I would eventually have the ammunition to support such cynicism?

I'd be lying if I said I didn't revert to a petulant teen myself and proclaim the unfairness of what went down. Yet through it all – the lack of power I had, the lack of compassion others had, the lack of sleep it all wrought – one inimitable fact remains: I never got a chance to say farewell. Talk about unfair. I wish I could tell you that I've made peace with this, that I understand that it had to be this way, and that it was all for the best. Nope. After all, I'm a teacher, not a prick in a suit. I'll spare you the rest. After all, you've got your own complaints to ready.

Farwell.

Mr. M.

Chapter 9

I remember being struck by how easy it had become to relay bad news to those I love. It was as effortless as sleeping or worrying. Pick up the phone. Go into contacts. Select one of the four names who have tolerated my immense burdens for months upon months. Assail them with the bleak particulars. Wait for their shock or pep talk. Repeat each step with remaining contacts.

My lack of details had to have elevated their frustration. But I saw no point in exploring the minutiae of what occurred at my Central Office meeting. The highlights were all that mattered. The attorney did all of the talking for the opposition. Not *most* of the talking. *All* of the talking. He asked me pointed question, all with a slight undertone of aggression in his voice. My answers were either candid admissions of what I had done wrong or lucid repudiations of the lies told by Martha and Aim, the woman who loves anagrams. T.J. and Tom, with laptops opened on the table in front of them, had their heads slightly bowed while Heather from HR typed away on her own computer. CEA Tom, and Steve the union rep., remained at my side, silent and deferential.

The Q&A lasted about fifteen minutes, after which I asked to make a statement. Allowing myself mere seconds to find a tone that straddled the line between contrition and conviction, I directed my monologue in the direction of my bosses. It went like this: "I take responsibility for opening my mouth when I shouldn't have, for breaching an investigation when I was asked to keep silent. And for that, I am truly sorry. But please know that I did not do it out of disrespect towards you or my coworkers in the English Department. I did it because I was driven by the two emotions that have been consuming me since January 7th of last year: fear and anxiety."

I told them I loved my job. I told them I *needed* my job, that I had two young children I was readying to likely lose their mother for at least a few years. I referenced a scene from the film *Doubt* where Philip Seymour Hoffman's character delivers a sermon about gossip, likening it to thousands of impossible to gather feathers from a pillow. My efforts had been futile, I admitted, in trying to locate and collect those feathers. And though they were plentiful in my case – the rumors and lies and accusations – I no longer wished to concern myself with any of it, I explained. It was all inconsequential at this point. I merely wished to return to work, and to my students, and teach literature like I had been doing for over a decade.

As I think back on my earnest attempt to show humility in search of decency, I can't help but wish I gave a different speech altogether. Maybe it's because a lot was left unsaid at that meeting. Or maybe it's because I now know the result of my efforts. Either way, I wish I stood up, scoffed a little, broke into a cool, slight grin, and said what I was too subservient to say:

"Focus all you want on the trivial. Focus all you want on my innocuous wrongdoing: breaching some investigation with no real weight to it in the first place. That doesn't negate matters of far greater consequence. Matters like me returning to work on January 8th to do my job. Matters like you providing me without a *single* guideline as to how I might deal with constantly seeing the kid who had his dick in my ex-wife's mouth. Or seeing the other kid who was the target of her grooming campaign – or teaching that kid's brother. There are other matters, too. There's me having to face my students day after day. No guidance there. None. And what about me having to interview a replacement for my ex-wife? And what about these petty, inane, transparent accusations brought forth by two of the most toxic people in the building, who also happen to be corresponding with my ex-wife? What about what's happened to my family? And to my children? What about the humiliation? The heartbreak? The unbelievable heartbreak? Shame on you. Shame on all of you. And not even for neglecting to mention any of this. But for thinking I am too stupid to not have noticed your neglect. I *have* noticed. How could I not? It is, after all, the crux of this matter. It is – contrary to what you believe. Your absurd investigation is meaningless. It's an illusion, a sophomoric card trick attempted on a grown man of more than reasonable intellect. It's a fucking insult is what it is. My presence here today is an insult. You making me grovel for my job is an insult. And I refuse to do so. So make whatever self-important decisions you feel you need to make before getting back to me. I'll be at home not giving a goddamn."

The reality is that they would have been as unmoved by this as they were by my actual speech. They had made up their minds prior to our April 20th meeting. To quote the district's lawyer: "All present parties feel it would be best if you pursued your professional endeavors elsewhere." I could have fought this. With the free attorney I was afforded by the district, I could have attempted to wear them down by costing them a lot of time and money. In the end, though, it would have amounted to either some last chance agreement or some perverse theatre of the absurd that would have only reinforced what we all knew to be the case: They had all the power and answers and authority.

CEA Tom apologized over and over once we reached the parking lot. Steve shook my hand and wished me luck.

"There's not much more I can tell you," I said to my parents and my sister and my tall, wild-haired girl.

Our shared reactions were typical. Disbelief. Disgust. A solemn sort of anger rooted in utter helplessness. It was hardly new terrain. The only difference this time around was I experienced a terrific marathon burst of desperate creativity. With nothing but time on my hands, I devoted four to five hours a day to writing. The urgency of my story increased with a violent-like spasm. I convinced myself that the end of my career at DHHS was the conclusion my book needed. It's true that at this point Allison's story had not yet played itself out. I didn't care. Reasoning that my own circumstances trumped hers, I summed up her ordeal by stating how her "fate is a mere Google search away." My foreword and two chapters eventually turned into a full length book. Telling myself the memoir would be my mission statement, my vindication, my revenge even, I wrote with no filter. The thought that I might offend or inflame or reveal too much never crossed my mind.

A handful of agents read that early draft. Though I received some hopeful feedback that the book was sellable, the consensus all around was that it was far too angry. One agent told me he needed aspirin upon finishing the manuscript. "Tone it down," he told me. "Tell your story, but lose the misery. No one wants to partake in that for a couple hundred pages." Shelving the book, I focused my efforts on finding a new job.

After sending resumes to a few surrounding districts, I went on some interviews and got an offer at a small high school twenty minutes from my home. The money was greater than what I had earned in Madison while the responsibilities were far less. My new bosses learned of my story, but told me they didn't care. As for the students I would eventually teach, most have backstories to rival my own. They are battered and beaten down by life. It would prove to be an ideal fit.

My ex-wife had become fascinated with the details of my professional life.

"I heard you lost your job," she said one morning when we exchanged the kids.

Ignoring her texts had become commonplace – and not terribly difficult to do. During this time, they were so often filled with either faux concern or bitter tidings. The messages would have to them a celebratory undertone that suggested I was in the nascent stages of coming undone and losing close to what she had lost. Yet dealing with her in person had proven more of a challenge. There seemed to be a fearlessness in her that might have stemmed from seeing my face, which she could read easily enough. My dread. My anxiety. It was hardly a mystery.

"You heard wrong," I told her.

"That's unlikely."

This was met with silence. It wouldn't be until the following week when I would provide her with some indication of how I was doing. It would be in the form of a brand new black Jeep Wrangler I bought on a whim. As juvenile as it was for me to revel in her seeing me and the kids pull up in our new car with the top off and the sun in our faces, it was equally effective in boasting about my continued survival.

As the summer of 2016 began, Allison sent me a text declaring that she would be enjoying her freedom through the fall and into the new year. Her lawyer had become adept at asking the court for continuances, all of which were granted. I began to envision the possibility that I would never have a reprieve from her – that I might never catch my breath, achieve inner peace, live with Robbie and Riley full time again. More daydreams of running away crept into my mind at the oddest of times. I would be folding laundry or playing beach wiffleball with the kids when thoughts of leaving the bullshit behind would practically overwhelm me. Hours were spent doing Google searches on small seaside towns down south. The thought of reinventing myself was both satisfying and overwhelming. I wrote a song during that time called "I Can't Stay." In it, I fused my loneliness and wanderlust and even tossed in a few lines about an upcoming high school reunion and some old friends I envied who had moved far away.

"I Can't Stay"

I can't believe I'm older now, but young enough to think I'm getting old
It's getting harder to relate to the mystery that is fate; it's easier turning silver into gold
I can't believe you moved out west and left me here to contemplate and muse
How all of my fair-weather friends turned their backs on me again and left me here without anything to lose

I can't stay much longer / And I can't stay out late
I'm wondering when you'll be home / And how long – just how long...I'll have to wait

The reunion's 'round the corner; it's coming up this fall in our hometown
I'll play my only hand...by singing with the band...we'll open every set with "Homeward Bound"

Things are getting easier; that's how it is when your castles have all
burned
And you find yourself knee-deep in trash, holding handfuls of blackened
ash
Tryin' to piece together all the lessons that you've learned

I can't stay much longer / And I can't stay out late
I'm wondering when you'll be home / And how long – just how
long...I'll have to wait

I can't stay / I'll get wrecked and wander away / Today

I can't believe it's over now / And everything is framed in black and
white
It's getting harder to relate to all the love that turns to hate / It's easier
turning darkness into light
I can't believe this loneliness / It whispers like a stranger on the street
Telling me I've stayed behind...and watched my memories go blind –
and left me here sitting at the mercy seat

I can't stay much longer / And I can't stay out late
I'm wondering when you'll be home / And how long – just how
long...I'll have to wait

A few weeks into the summer, I published an excerpt of this book in
Coastal Connecticut. Coastal, for which I have been a regular
contributor for years, is a tasteful magazine of artsy events and local
happenings. On occasion, they will throw in some literary pieces from
local authors. When Owen, my editor, asked if I had any ideas for
contributions, I suggested something from *Land of July*. He was
certainly familiar with my story, as well as the book I had been working
on. After revising one particular excerpt, I sent it off and waited for a
reply. Owen responded within a few days, telling me he would proudly
publish what I had sent. So in the summer 2016 issue, amidst recipes for
seasonal sangria and pieces with breezy nautical themes, was my *Land of*

July excerpt.

"So you're writing a book?" Allison said to me one morning when she dropped off the kids.

"Yes."

"Do you think that's a good idea?"

"I think it's my right to share this godforsaken story from my own point of view."

"For what purpose?"

"I'm not entirely sure right now."

"Will you please reconsider? I don't think it's a smart move."

All I could think of was her mother's reaction a few years earlier when Allison began therapy. The thought of others learning such intimate familial details was too much for her to bear. It would be empowering to say that I responded with something confident and definitive, something like, "I make zero apologies for writing this book. Zero. I'm writing it and I can promise it will see the light of day. And even though I'm not entirely sure right now as to why I've chosen to share this appalling story, I am committed to doing so." The truth is that I had reservations about writing the book. Was it in poor taste to do so? Was it exploitative? Was it somehow an affront to Robbie and Riley?

Despite these misgivings, I continued to write. The story was still playing itself out and I felt I had no choice but to chronicle it in all its madness. *Land of July* became a way for me to collect the moments, past and present, that stopped me in my tracks, a way to sort through the ongoing drama that seemed ceaseless. It went beyond trying to achieve a catharsis. I found that I was sincerely intrigued by what was happening.

That summer my children told me about their mother's new friend, a man named Ed who had replaced Jeremy. Ed had met Allison in the grocery store one afternoon; phone numbers were quickly exchanged with the promise of a future get-together. According to Robbie and Riley, Ed visited the apartment the next day. He apparently stayed for hours while managing to have a few make-out sessions with Allison.

When I asked my ex-wife about this, imploring her to use discretion in front of the kids, she told me to mind my own business. It occurred to me that her thinking was similar to what it had been months earlier, back before her crimes were discovered – that I was jealous. With as much deference as I could manage, I asked her again to keep such scenes from the kids. She scoffed at this. The struggle to impart simple, common-sense principles to this woman I had known for so long became an impossibility. In the best of times, she had proven impervious to what I had to say. Yet now, with the divorce behind us, I had the feeling that she was flaunting her singleness in my face, positive she owed me nothing in the way of an explanation for anything she did.

On August 25, I attended a birthday dinner at L'Orcio's in New Haven for my tall, wild-haired girl. Her parents would be there, as well as some of her siblings. It was a lovely summer evening and we had a 6:30 reservation on the patio. We were drinking white wine and making small talk when I was suddenly kicked underneath the table by my tall, wild-haired girl. Her expression was fixated on whatever was going on behind me. When I turned around, I was met with the sight of the hostess attempting to seat Allison and her date, a man with a full head of gray hair who looked old enough to be her father. When she saw us, she smiled and waved. Then she asked the hostess for a different table, one on the other side of the patio, which happened to be perfectly within my line of sight. I later found out that her date, a man named Chris A., happened to be one of her bosses; Chris is not only a Madison resident, but Allison previously taught both of his children. I also learned from a friend that she was seeing a nineteen-year-old college student from SCSU. There was no choice but to text her, asking that she please not bring any of her men around my children, stating how it was obvious that she had no meaningful relationships with these people. She responded by sending me a YouTube link of Dolly Parton singing "I Will Always Love You." The following day, she would send another text, addressing another matter altogether.

"The kids and I are in Florida. They're so excited. Be home in a few."

"Are you kidding me?"

"Nope."

"You flew?"

"Yup. The kids had a blast during the flight."

"You took my kids on a plane, left the state, and withheld this information from me until now."

"I asked my lawyer about it and I'm perfectly within my rights."

"We both know what this is: your last hurrah. Enjoy it."

When I contacted Ray Hassett, he recommended we file a motion against her. He asked me to send him my concerns. Leading my list was the Florida trip as well as the litany of men she might be exposing my children to.

"It's good to have a paper trail," Ray said. "You never know when it'll come in handy."

The summer ended with a face-to-face meeting between my ex-wife and I. After she dropped the kids off one morning, she asked if we could speak for a few moments on my front porch. The conversation began by Allison telling me she was notified by her lawyer about the motion I had filed.

"It wasn't necessary to do that."

"Talking to you has become pointless," I said. "Which is why it's best to go through the lawyers."

"Rob, I'm still the same person. I'm still your girl. I haven't changed. I know you think I'm a monster, but I'm not. I'm the same girl you married."

Her face was flush with a sort of willful desperation to convince me of this. At its core, though, it was nothing more than a capricious statement; the truth is that if I told her to fuck off, she would have morphed into a lunatic right before my eyes. It became obvious to me what was at play: Her time was running out. The summer was ending and she would soon be faced with going to trial or accepting a plea deal for her crimes.

"I'd like it if things could be peaceful between us," she went on. "It's in the kids' best interest."

"Your behavior is destructive," I told her. "And until it's not, peace between us will be impossible."

"My behavior is not destructive."

"You don't see it. You *can't* see it. You never could. You're blinded by something. I'm not sure what it is, but it's one hell of a force."

"I know who I am. I'm a good person."

"I'm not really interested in your distorted self-views. Save them for your therapist."

"I have awareness."

"If you had any awareness, you'd recognize what you've done as otherworldly, and you don't."

She crinkled up her forehead a little and repeated the word I had used: "otherworldly."

"Odd word choice," she said, the trace of a grin creeping onto her lips.

I shrugged and asked if she had anything more to say. She told me she did. And then she said something that was so spot on and pitch perfect in proving my point that it left me speechless.

"I just want you to know that other female teachers at DHHS also found Gabe and Zach attractive."

When fall began, just days into my new teaching position, I published the second excerpt to *Land of July*. I wrote, worked, raised my kids, played music, and awaited the outcome to Allison's case, which had begun twenty months earlier.

Dear Marriage,

With your storied history and rich pageantry, you come across as something truly divine. You claim you stand for commitment and security and love and the hope of a bright, wide future.

Oh, how you misrepresent yourself. You appear honorable, like a clergyman decked out in his finery. But you are no clergyman. In fact, you're closer to a white collar criminal, sitting there in your lavish office, a beguiling grin plastered on your face while contemplating your offshore accounts and your pristine Mercedes for which you paid cash. On paper, you seem to make perfect sense. But you're as convoluted as a pyramid scheme.

Do I sound melodramatic? Ill informed? Just plain insane? Is it not you who causes so much destruction and heartbreak, but we, the people? Are we too sensitive, too selfish, too stupid to enter into your domain? Have we not evolved enough to be able to handle the colossal responsibilities you demand? Perhaps. But that doesn't discount the fact that you, like some sadistic Nazi doctor, pick and choose those on whom you wish to conduct your experiments.

Excuse me if I sound like I'm victimizing myself. I don't mean to. I suppose it's just that I feel like I'm stranded somewhere and holding in my hand a misshapen clump of my past, trying desperately to see something of worth in it that inspires me to be a bright-eyed optimist. Sound corny? Well Christ, I'd like to impart to my children that they shouldn't pack up their belongings and run from you like you were the devil himself. But I suppose I did just a moment ago compare you to a Nazi doctor, didn't I?

I honestly don't even know if I care all that much that you're a hack, a punchline, a novelty gag. Maybe some days I do and some days I don't. Just like some days I'll blame you and all your archaic limitations and some days I'll blame the people. Either way, I suppose, the joke is on me.

Rob

Chapter 10

Anyone tuned in to Allison's court appearances had to have grown weary. A new date had been scheduled every four to six weeks for close to two years, making justice appear remote and elusive. The victim's families must have been as confounded as I was. My mother, who attended more than half those court dates, was growing especially restless. With as much restraint as she could muster, she sent a letter to the prosecution, asking if the continuances would soon cease and when we might expect closure. The response she received was polite but vague. The court did not name me and my children as interested parties in the case, which seemed another injustice altogether.

"I can't believe you're not seen as victims," my mother would say. "It makes no sense."

As troubled as I was over my ex-wife's continued freedom, and how she seemed to flaunt that freedom in my face, I had grown inured to the arrangement. My interest in her fate and in justice prevailing was becoming obsolete. What would occasionally make it topical were the many inquiries put to me on Allison's behalf; it had been about two years and people began to grow suspicious that the Madison teacher fired and arrested for sexual misconduct just might have gotten away with everything. I therefore found myself becoming the occasional spokesman for righteousness.

"It's imminent," I'd tell anyone who asked me about it. "I can't say when, but it's got to be soon."

Nothing at first seemed notable about Allison's November 28th court appearance. That is until Robbie and Riley announced to me that their grandmother, Allison's mother, would be coming down from New Brunswick the week before to stay with her daughter.

"This is it," my mother predicted. "It has to be. It's been long enough."

Her prediction was right. I was in the middle of a band rehearsal when a text came through telling me what had happened. The judge presiding over the case, Melanie Cradle, gave a recommended sentence of three years in prison. The offer was to either accept the deal and begin serving time on March 3rd, 2017, or else take it to trial. The latter was a laughable prospect. Exorbitant legal costs aside, the mountains of evidence against her seemed to dictate that we finally had a finish line we could begin contemplating. Upon hearing this news, my insides suddenly felt hollow. Whatever revenge I had been seeking, whatever relief I was counting on, was now elusive. I went to bed that evening thinking about the sheer dread that must have been multiplying every minute inside Allison's brain.

The groundwork needed to be laid for Robbie and Riley. I was a proponent for the least dramatic approach. No long, drawn-out discussions. No histrionics. No elaborate explanations. Most importantly, no use of the word "jail." My idea was simple: It involved telling the kids their mom was going to a rehab facility for a time to think about some mistakes she had made. She would be safe and close by and would call a few times a week. I checked with Allison to see if we might collaborate on this.

"I don't want to lie to them," she said.

"Neither do I."

"Then I think we should tell them everything."

"That *is* everything. But we're favoring euphemism rather than blunt reality. They're five and nine."

"I think we need to tell them I'm going to jail."

"Jail is a dark fantasy world to them. It's pretend. Make believe. It doesn't exist outside of games and movies. I'm not interested in giving them nightmares."

Allison told me she would think about it. She said she needed to consult some experts on the matter and get back to me. But she agreed that unity was the best strategy and promised me she would not go rogue.

Within the week she would tell them she was going to jail because she "talked to some boys Daddy didn't like." Another call was made to my attorney who asked once again for me to elucidate my concern. I did so, and the paper trail continued.

The next few months were filled with bizarre efforts on Allison's part to be conciliatory. They were as capricious as they were too late to be effective. She sent me well wishes on Christmas and told me she still loved me. She invited me and my tall, wild-haired girl to her apartment for a New Year's get together. She recorded herself singing an a cappella rendition of Tom Petty's "Wildflowers" and sent it to my iPhone. There was the "Happy Birthday" text and the "I'm sorry David Bowie died" text. There was the YouTube link to Joni Mitchell's "A Case of You." There was a somber update that a former student of ours from the Grove School had passed.

There was little mystery. Each text was an attempt to connect, to remember, to be human, to build some makeshift bridge out of whatever fossils she could find, no matter how foreign or flimsy they might have been. I responded to none of them, knowing full well that a mercurial despair lay beneath the surface that might have been penetrating in its realness, but was likely just as dangerous. Instead, I pitied her from afar and felt nothing but disgust that I had such little control over this instinct.

Whatever nostalgia I had left in me was transitory. As for my memories of Allison, they were in absolute ruins. I had to force myself into an almost trancelike state to conjure even fragments of a life I knew we lived, but could scarcely recall. My family surmised that it was a case of my brain protecting me. I began reading about neuroscience and PTSD and Freud's theory of repression. My goal was not to stave off further memory loss, but to come to terms with what had happened to my mind. As sad as it might have been that I was robbed of the ability to ruminate on years of a life together, I was grateful to have all but forgotten. I know we went to Virginia Beach and Mexico and Atlanta when we were a newly married couple. I know we bought and sold a lot of homes and I know we worked together as teachers for years. I know I entertained her with a character I named Ernie who spoke with a lisp and could never get a fact straight. I know we had two children and that we saw John Hiatt and Ryan Adams in concert and that we planted a garden that grew more tomatoes and cucumbers than we knew what to do with. There's empirical proof of all of this, but no other kind. And who wants to deal in practicality when asking whether moments in their life were worthwhile?

If I was fixated on any period time, it was on a single day. January 6th, 2015. The day before Allison's crimes were discovered. A week earlier, we hosted a New Year's Eve party. It was one of our better gatherings. The house was bursting with drunken friends and delicious food. I put Robert Palmer's *Sneakin' Sally Through the Alley* album on repeat. A few days ahead was my fortieth birthday. But as for January 6th, it's an utter blank in my mind – a cobweb wiped out with a single, giant sweeping motion. I think about that day. It was a Tuesday. It was winter. The details I want to learn would now prove useless. I know this. But still. I'm curious. Curious about what I wore and what music I listened to during my drive to work. Curious about conversations between me and Allison and how we entertained our children that evening. I want to know what we had for dinner and what we talked about as we ate. I'd like to know about my sleep that night and if my dreams gorged themselves on something fantastical or humdrum. I can't help but wonder about Allison and if she felt a constant hovering sense of dread that she would soon be found out, and that the results would be a category five hurricane. There's also the curiosity over what we shared with one another throughout those twenty-four hours, and if there might have been some tenderness between us. Anything at all. A compliment. An embrace. A reminiscence. Intimacy. Laughter. Something genuine and not just born out of her fear. It's hard to say. Fifty-fifty, I suppose.

As March 3rd approached, I found myself considering the strands of my story that would signify its ending. Some fell into my lap and were so conspicuous in their need to be part of this narrative. Others were far murkier. Here's a conspicuous one: A third victim of my ex-wife's came forward. Along with one of her original boys, he and his family have filed suit against her. It would be fitting to say that I was shocked

194

upon learning this, that I hung my head in disbelief and felt a fresh sting from yet another hideous betrayal. But I did not. Nor did I reexamine our marriage or her disloyalty or my naïveté. I had arrived, it seemed, at the road of indifference. Finally. It took long enough. Remarkable how that happens. It slips into the bloodstream like a narcotic and you can't feel a thing. It's painless and perfect in all its wooziness.

Another conspicuous one: Martha and Allison began taking dance classes together. I only mention this because how could I not? My source in finding it out is credible. Like a young child taking a nasty spill, this is either hilarious or heartbreaking. There's certainly a visual there. And a motive as well. Perhaps I'll appear selfish reading into this, but I can't help but feel that each step they took was a celebratory one, exultant over the chance that I was crawling through mud, wiping furiously at my eyes, trying like hell to see an inch in front of me to some clear path that would give me at least a moment to catch my breath. I can't help but contemplate the thinking that went into Martha's decision to register for the class, pay the money, and devote at least one night a week to socializing with a former coworker who was fired for such appalling reasons. I've certainly heard of running from your problems, but never dancing from them. At times, this appeared to me to be an act of subterfuge, some jubilant distraction from Allison's ineffable reality. Other times it seemed almost graceful in how far removed it was from the tragedy that had become her life. It shows a certain strength and will that I'm not at all sure I possess.

The murkier strands involve a lot of difficult questions. Will I remain in Madison? Will I ever forgive Allison? Will I marry again? Will Robbie and Riley be okay? Will I someday give them this book to read? Right now, it's 8:25 a.m. on a Wednesday and I know the answer to all of these. I am confident and resolute and I can explain myself in great detail. But I'm positive that yesterday, at around noon, each of these questions would have stumped me. Now it's 8:27 a.m. and I find myself once again at a loss for answers.

Here are some more: Why does this book even exist? Did I really *have* to write it? What's it actually about? What am I hoping to gain? Couldn't I have done what my former employers wanted me to do?

Couldn't I have just shut my mouth and moved forward and respected the mores of polite society by reconciling with the past? Absolutely not. Asking me to keep my mouth shut about this ghastly story makes as much sense to me as it would to ask a cartographer to ignore a certain stretch of road and wipe it away forever from every map ever produced. Okay, so I branded the world with my ugly tattoo. But even ugly tattoos, with a careful hand and some inspired vision, can be turned into something lovely.

As for the other questions, there's a bit more to say on them – in no particular order. This book is about a family and a life that almost was. Over the years it came close here and there, but never really caught on. It's about the two saddest sentences in the world: "Now that summer's over" and "Now that the kids are grown." I think about these sentences all the time. I have to plan for their occasions more than I ever did before. I have to gather an arsenal of supplies and anticipate battle. It's not going to be pretty; that's for sure. But I tell myself that my basic training has prepared me well. We'll see about that.

Yes, there will be new summers. I tell this to my children every year. "It's a no brainer," I say to them. "Just count the days. Check a calendar. Look ahead." But there's still a mourning process. This is reasonable. When you're a kid, when you have kids, when you're a teacher, summer transcends being just a season. It's freedom. It's fireworks. It's a delicious promise of memories and magic and probably the closest any of us will ever come to learning the absolute potential of a family.

As for when Robbie and Riley are grown, that's another matter. That's more *my* concern. I look forward to it with both dread and delight. Yet another no brainer. Just count the days. Check a calendar. Look ahead. I do. Then I don't. I can't. Some days this is beyond unbearable. Others I manage just fine.

This book is about the vows we make to one another in our lifetime. These vows take on different forms. Some are spoken and some are silent. Some we will write out in the sand and some are merely hinted at with the rarest of smiles. My vows have been songs for as long as I can remember. This form suits me. I can eschew sentimentality and

196

be playful or cryptic if I need to be. Any vow, whether it's a song or a love letter, will last for as long as we believe in it by turning it into a one act play we can handle with reasonable overhead. No theatre. No props. No extras.

Over the years, I have offered vows to nearly everyone I love. This includes my children and my family and people from my past and my tall, wild-haired girl. And although Allison is now and forever a stranger to me, I know I will continue to offer my vows to her. In fact, I just finished a brand new song the other day. It's called "The Ballad of Your Final Epic Disaster." It has lines in it like "Your secrets aren't safe, I've laid them to waste, the neighbors know just what you did. It's time to come clean, and confront your old dreams, it's time to sit down and tell the kids."

Whatever songs I was going to write prior to January 7th, 2015, are now and forever abandoned. But there are plenty of new ones waiting in the wings. Some will have a great sense of urgency to them. Some will be caustic. Some will be cruel. But all will be honest and born with a halo of hard luck around them.

As March 3rd came into focus, the strands kept coming. Allison told me that in an effort to prepare for prison, she would be selling her possessions and giving up her apartment.

"I'll be bringing the kids' things by in the next few days," she said.

"Where will you be staying once your apartment is gone."

"A hotel."

"Where?"

"I'm not sure."

"Please let me know when you decide."

"Why? So you can send the media there?"

"So I can know where my children are staying."

Allison's mother arrived in the states a few days before March 3rd. Together, they packed up clothes and toys and books and movies and deposited them on my front lawn while I was at work. I would arrive home to stacks of boxes that I would drag inside my garage. After slicing through the packing tape with my car key, I'd pour through the contents of each box, marveling over how my children wanted for nothing. What especially struck me was how sickening it must have been for their mother to streamline their things, pack them up, and deliver them to my house. Her devastations were surely in the double digits – the losses, the humiliation, the uncertainty of her future – and these deliveries had to have made the list.

When I reached out again to ask about the hotel, I was ignored. I persisted. She refused to tell me. The lawyers became involved. A warning letter was written, threatening to involve the police. In the end, her obstinacy won out and I had no choice but to hope that Robbie and Riley would be safe with Allison, whose freedom was growing more precarious by the minute.

My mother began to fear I might lash out and land myself in trouble.

"Let her have these little victories," she said. "It's all she has left."

"That doesn't make it any less maddening."

"Just wait it out. It'll all be over with soon enough."

"I'm going to court on March 3rd," I said.

"Where is this coming from?"

This was a valid question. Never before did I have any intention of witnessing this final spectacle. The thought of it was grotesque. There did exist a spiteful desire to attend the March 3rd session where I'd secure a front row seat to watch my ex-wife squirm as she was read the riot act by Judge Cradle before being handcuffed and led away in tears to some holding cell in a quiet, windowless room. But this was nothing more than a dark daydream. What prevailed was my need to steer clear from the entire affair. Until something in me changed. It might have been a need for closure, or a simple case of my fantasy transforming into reality.

"I'm not sure," I said. "I just think I need to be there. Save me a seat."

"I think this will be good for you," my mother said. "It'll be hard, but cathartic. It's all coming to a close. Two miserable years. Yet a much needed reprieve is in sight."

Then she reminded me of the text messages between Allison and her victims. A motion had been filed some time back for this evidence to be shared with me once the case was concluded. The hope was that we might use what we suspected would be a keen glimpse into her psyche for a future custody battle.

March 3rd. It was a Friday. I took the day off. Robbie and Riley stayed with their mother and grandmother the previous night. Though Allison kept their whereabouts a secret, I texted her a number of times, imploring her to keep her composure in front of the kids. I tried to imagine their goodbye when she dropped them off in the morning. It would be close to three years before she would see them again. Robbie would be in junior high school, combating hormones and social cliques. Riley would be coming into her own as well, no doubt thrilling her teachers with her wit and precociousness.

The sentencing was scheduled for 9:00 a.m. At 8:30, I drove to Island Avenue Elementary School where I asked the secretary to pull Robbie and Riley from their classrooms. We found a quiet corner in the hallway where we talked and embraced one another. They were both in surprisingly good spirits. My intention was to take them home and scrap going into New Haven if they turned out to be distressed. Since they told me they were okay, I hugged and kissed them and told them I would see them after school.

By the time I made it to the courthouse, my adrenaline was palpable. It seemed impossible that this day had finally arrived. It dawned on me that for some time, during the battles and the bullshit, the heartbreak and the humiliation, I was going through a process to prepare myself that Allison was going to prison. It also occurred to me that her own process must have been akin to the world's slowest evisceration. There were goodbyes upon goodbyes and the selling off of possessions and the surrendering of power and autonomy and freedom and the constant reexamination of just how in the hell all of this could have happened.

I was reminded again of just how austere the New Haven courthouse is. With its white marble and cavernous spaces, joy cannot be found within an inch of the place, and it's next to impossible, no matter how deserving one feels they are, to manufacture even the most infinitesimal bit. I found my mother in the lobby and we made our way into courtroom C on the first floor.

"This is where the heavy duty cases go down," she whispered to me as we took our front row seats.

The room was packed. Faces were drawn. Talk was soft and somber as people moved up and down the aisles to get the view they wanted. Once all the seats were taken, it grew silent. Two bailiffs paced up and down in front of the judge's bench. Allison was nowhere to be found. After a minute, my mother nudged me and motioned to the rear of the courtroom. When I turned around, I saw Janice, my ex-mother-in-law. With her white, stringy, shoulder-length hair, and her plump face all blotchy and solemn, she looked absolutely ancient. Seated next to her was a woman named Melissa with whom Allison had formed a friendship at the inception of her debacle.

In a matter of a few more minutes, Allison entered the courtroom. At her side was her attorney, a weathered looking man with a gangly frame and a full head of white hair. They moved to the front and center of the floor, directly in front of the judge's bench. I felt the silence of the room crawl inside my gut and wreak havoc on my organs. In her white pants and gray shawl, Allison stood upright and still, careful to keep from turning around to face her audience. Her lawyer whispered to her a few times and rubbed her back. I thought about the need she had her entire life for a father figure. Clayton, her biological father, had always proven unstable and unreliable. Billy, her step-father, was as childlike as he was chronically absent from family life due to long, arduous hours as a laborer for a power company. Both had been in Canada, over six hundred miles away, for the past fifteen or so years. As for my own father, he loved her like a daughter. They had an immediate rapport, which lasted until the bitter end. It could be said that my entire family embraced Allison without reservation. Yet the many years, the meals and holidays shared, the bonds and confidences forged, ended up amounting to nothing. She never so much as sent them an email saying mea culpa, or I'm sorry, or perhaps most saliently, goodbye.

When the bailiff announced Judge Cradle's entrance into the courtroom from her chambers, everyone rose from their seats. After some preliminary statements, as well as stern warnings to keep all cell phones off and out of sight, the hearing had begun. An advocate for the victim's families asked that the court allow readings from the parents of the victims. First up was Gabe's father. In a quavering voice, he read from a script he unfolded from his shirt pocket. He said how his son had been victimized and humiliated by someone who should have had his best interests at heart. He talked about how his son had to transfer schools and that he suffered from PTSD from the ordeal, and how he was stigmatized and was bound to have troubled relationships for much of his life. My mother, who began to softly weep, latched onto my hand. The speech lasted about five minutes. Five minutes of candid and heartbreaking sentiments that were disturbing to hear, yet hardly difficult to believe.

Next up was Zach's plight. This monologue, written by his mother, was read by the advocate for the families. It was far longer and much more caustic than the previous one. It referred to Allison as sick and disturbed and said how her breach of the teacher/student relationship was unforgivable. Zach's mother claimed that Allison was a predator and never once seemed sorry for what she had done and that she was deserving of her punishment. She went on to talk about the difficulties her son was having after what had happened to him: sleeplessness, shame, thoughts of suicide. My eyes were fixated on Allison as she stood there with no choice but to listen to what she had done to these teenagers, to their futures, to their families. Two years had passed since her crimes were found out; in that time, I thought often on whether she had the slightest awareness of who the true victims actually were. All interactions between she and I suggested she was too myopic to see beyond how her own life had been affected. Even at this moment, there was nothing to indicate true contrition. Her body language was static. There was no movement, no deep breaths, no tears.

Allison's lawyer was the next to speak. Addressing the judge, he stated how his client was interested only in moving forward in her life and that she was eager to pay her debt to society and someday be reunited with her children. In a dramatic turn, he said how no one in this world may lay claim to the moral high ground and how his client made some mistakes, yet was on the road to a higher place of understanding and was committed to making the best of her time in prison. He then went on to state how Allison was troubled at the time of her crimes, citing the suicide of a friend as well as an unsupportive husband. My mother squeezed my hand. I shook my head and waited for the finale, which came soon enough with the judge reading off the convictions and accompanying sentences. Two counts of Unlawful Restraint in the 1st degree: 360 days each. Two counts of Reckless Endangerment in the 2nd degree: 180 days each. One count of Threatening in the 2nd degree: 360 days. One count of Harassment in the 2nd degree: 15 days.

The bailiffs then escorted Allison and her attorney to a back room. The spectators rose and filed out, still solemn and deferential. The immediate aftermath of witnessing such a scene had with it such strains of awkwardness. I was unclear as to what to say, how to be, where to go. I opted to hug my mother and drive home to meet my children who would soon be returning from school.

•   •   •   •   •

In my mind, the days and weeks that were to follow were destined to be tranquil. I would reunite with Robbie and Riley full time and take a deep sigh that we could move on with our lives. I would focus solely on being a parent, a homemaker, a teacher. I was looking forward to my thoughts taking on new dimensions, ones that were free from the violent bends made by chaos and depression and uncertainty. What I found instead was that I was consumed with a brand new burden: coping with two young children who had lost their mother to one of the most unnatural causes imaginable. With that burden came a fresh kind of hatred I began to feel towards Allison. This time around, the hatred was of the quieter brand. It no longer had strident schemes of retribution. It was shapeless and without direction.

Yet for all my newfound angst, Robbie and Riley were no worse for wear. They continued to thrive in every way. In the spring, Robbie made AAA in baseball, the more competitive Little League. He continued to be a force in his martial arts class. Riley got a perfect report card, and started gymnastics, a sport for which she seemed destined. Our bond together had grown even stronger. The three of us had run amok through an unbelievable battlefield for twenty-six months and now we had come home to lick our wounds and help each other heal. The legal system didn't recognize us as victims, and they didn't need to. This is fine. We know what we've been through. And what we'll continue to go through. It defies labels.

Within a few weeks of Allison being gone, I received an email from my attorney telling me I had some documents to pick up at the Madison Police Department. Leaving work early, I stopped by the station, put $116 on my credit card, and drove home with a bundle of papers that must have been three inches thick. When I called my mother to tell her what I had, she warned me to brace myself as I read them.

"This is the last piece," she told me. "Those texts will give you more insight into her betrayal and state of mind than you ever thought possible. They're going to be a tough read. Have a bottle of wine on hand as you go through them. Call me when you finish."

I took her advice on the wine and opened a cheap bottle of Sauvignon. Then I sat on my front porch for close to two hours and read word for word what had transpired between Allison and her teenage victims a couple years back. I found myself drifting from one role to another as I read: One minute I was a feckless cuckold up to my neck in disgust, and the next I was an amateur psychoanalyst who was riveted by the motives of someone who could do and say such vile things with her underage pupils.

Throughout the hundreds of pages of texts, Allison expertly played the role of predator, victim, and seductress. There was a conversation about her getting one of the boys off, and another one about how she liked to be told what to do while naked, and one where she invited Zach to our house late one night while I was out with my band and while Robbie and Riley were asleep. There were texts that showed her practically begging for attention. These were perhaps more disturbing than the lurid ones. Her tenacity was peerless to the point of being abusive. Especially with Gabe. There are moments between the two where he tries to sever their union, but she presses him and guilts him and goads him. At one point, he tells her that he is a teenage boy and that he owes her nothing and wants no further communication. Yet she couldn't resist. In her last text message to Gabe, sent on September 17th, mere weeks into the 2014 school year, she confesses that she is in love with him. He never responded.

My mother was right in how she viewed the texts: They did manage to be the final piece of the story. They brought me full circle to the point in time when Allison's deception was at its peak. Reading those few hundred pages was the closest I would ever come to screwing off the top of her head and getting a good look inside. I began to wonder how close her insidious thoughts were to her normal ones. They must have lived side by side, sharing a common space, each given equal credence. Thoughts as pedestrian as what to eat and wear and how lovely the weather was must have been terrified by the much darker fare staring it square in the face.

Like some self-proclaimed sleuth, I read the texts over and over again, searching for something more sophisticated than what was evident: a damaged middle-aged woman shining daylight on her basest desires, thinking somehow she was impervious to boundaries and law. I always observed the dates of the texts, knowing full well they were written when our two children and I were right under her nose.

Aside from giving me voyeuristic privileges no one wants, the texts also ignited a revelation that seemed at first modest, but soon grew in stature in my mind: Allison had turned on me. From the onset of our tragedy, I recognized the obvious, which was that she had cheated on me, humiliated me, devastated me. But the texts made me see how she had turned on me. This smacked of far greater consequence. She had taken every vow she had ever made to me, to our children, to herself even, and made a mockery of them. She held something that no alchemy could ever forge and dangled it over a jagged cliff before watching it fall from her grasp, all the while grinning like a madwoman.

The texts were inspirational in a demented sort of way; they coaxed from me a nine-page letter I wrote to Allison. Coming in at 4114 words, the letter was incendiary. My plan was to shock her with truths about who she really was and what she had done and how her only salvation was to admit that she was utterly lost and without even a trace of rationale for her actions. I ranted and pleaded and spewed bombastic diatribes about everything sacrosanct and everything obliterated by her ruthless vanity. The tender parts I included – mostly reminiscences – were intended to balance out an otherwise vitriolic letter. My plan was to mail the letter to York Correctional Institution. Yet I soon rethought this, opting to use it instead as a coda for this book. Yet that idea was abandoned when it instantly struck me who my bittersweet finale had to invoke. So I let the letter linger, dormant and inert somewhere in the cloud. I've read it now probably a dozen or more times. It exhausts me each time. On more than one occasion I've come close to deleting it altogether. Yet something compels me to hold on to it. I'm not entirely sure why, but I have a feeling I may need it in the future.

Today, everything is different. And yet nothing is. I'm at once more cynical and hopeful. I may be less romantic, yet I'm more giving. Life is more complicated these days, but I find I'm drawn to simplicity more than ever. I'm less than I was since January 7th, 2015, but I marvel when I think about the fresh swells of ecstatic delight living inside of me. I'm far more dramatic. But less vocal. Which is why I thank God for writing. Writing allows me to force solitude upon myself and flesh out these contradictions. When I hit my stride, I can trace their origin and direction and sometimes even assume a little control over them. I can continue my search for what in this life is steadfast and what is fleeting. It's a search that is both beloved and cursed. And it's one that I know will always lead me in some way to those two sad sentences about summer being gone and the kids being grown.

The search also leads me to the voices of Robbie and Riley – voices so pure and wise that I find I often force myself to dream about them. They tell me so much, those voices. Everything, really. And there's nothing I can't understand as they do their mightiest to fill my head with notions that are as clear as rainwater. They tell me about who they are and what they want to be. They tell me what's worth their time these days and why. They tell me about love and loyalty and even forgiveness. They are busy fashioning their own vows to themselves and to those they love.

A lot of this changes from week to week and month to month.

Some of it does, anyway. But some of it remains the same. And always will. Like the Land of July. That's unchanging. The place. The state of mind. The bedtime story. My children know this. That's why they smile whenever it's brought up. Not a beaming sort of smile. But a slight one. One that is modest, respectful even. It's as if they understand the need to bring it up. And to *keep* bringing it up. It doesn't matter if it's me who brings it up or if it's them. They're spellbound all the same. It just needs to continue to be brought up. That's important. It's as important as vows made and broken. It's as important as what's possible in this world, or what's out there for us to dream of or talk about with awe and reverence; it's as important as screwing up our eyes to get a good look into the future, and not minding whether we do so out of necessity or obligation, or whether it's a discipline or state of mind, but recognizing that however we may look ahead, we do so like our lives absolutely depend on it. Because in a lot of way they do.

Afterword

This memoir has been heavily edited. Its original draft was over fifty pages longer. At the urging of some, I've eliminated entire sections, chapters even. One such omission is what I referred to as my "built-in soundtrack." My original idea was to begin each chapter with an in-depth look at one of the many records I purchased during my ordeal. These bits, which were contemplative and perhaps even a bit dreamy, were hard to cut. Yet they were far too esoteric and probably self-indulgent to make the final draft. It's true that they helped reveal my wayward sorrow, but they compromised the narrative, which left me no choice but to delete them. Below is a taste of what I begrudgingly excised:

If author Raymond Carver sang and played an instrument, he might have written songs like what Dawes have come up with for their fourth record, All Your Favorite Bands. The characters on the album are burnt out, lost, isolated; they're coasting through their melancholy with low expectations and a heart full of hope. What they want – solace, affection, to be thought of fondly, to have their love given a full panoramic view of everlasting possibility – is not at all unreasonable.

Yet they know that the chances of getting any of this are as sparse as the songs' arrangements.

The song that lends its title to the name of the album is perhaps the most hopeful. Its lyrics include lines like "I hope your brother's El Camino runs forever / I hope the world sees the same person that you've always been to me / And may all your favorite bands stay together." Once the romantic grandeur of this metaphor gets vacuumed up by the maelstrom of reality, all that remains are the brittle bones of impossible potential. Does the song square off with Robert Frost's sentiment that "nothing gold can stay," or is it a mere throwaway? The answer is obvious. The song is simply a wish, a champagne toast. It's not made in earnest to come true. And it sure as hell isn't destined to. It's just a nice thought. Nothing more. Yes, the bands will break up. Or simply dissolve. All of them. We all know this. But first they'll feud and fuck each other over and welsh on their debts to one another and slander each member and steal shit when others aren't looking and become exhausted and bitter and broken. Some members will form new bands. Some will go solo. Some will retire. Some will mourn the loss forever. Some will get over it before the checks are cashed. Some will pretend they're over it. Some will pretend successfully. Some unsuccessfully.

As for me, I want it all to last forever. I always have. I want to share a communal house with every person I've ever loved. I want to vacation a few times a year with my childhood. I want to skid across hot coals with my adolescence. I want to take my family when they're young and healthy and walk down the aisle with them to renew our vows to one another, me and my children leading the way, their arms interlocked with mine, their big, gorgeous eyes all full of the future, so delicious and so malleable.

This now seems like part of what could be a different book altogether. It could be titled *Nine Albums that Helped Save My Life*. Perhaps I'll get around to writing it one of these days. I do like the idea – especially after enough time has passed, allowing me the perspective to see how it best functions as a separate entity from the rest of *Land of July*.

Aside from my precious little music musings, *Land of July*, in its original draft, had far more anger, bitterness, and expletives than its final published form. I can recall one publisher telling me point blank over the phone that reading the memoir to him was "like reading a detailed accident report of carnage and catastrophe that left nothing out and nothing to the imagination." Before we parted ways, he added that the book's catharsis needed to be something other than just my act of writing it.

My conviction was such that I swore I wouldn't change a single word. My reasoning was simple: This is an honest account of what happened, as well as an honest telling of how it made me *feel*. The book was an enormous spittoon of sorts, and one into which I spat everything I felt and thought and wanted and hated and feared. My five senses were absolutely awash in my own tragedy. The nadir of my suffering seemed to occur daily. It became the essence of every exchange I had, and certainly everything I wrote. Yet time went by. And with it came more than a few rejections of my book, many of which pointed out its excess of vitriol. Stripping the story down, shaping it into something readable and hopefully relatable on some level, providing the reader with an opportunity for catharsis, of course became my objectives.

There's no denying that there's still some venom in these pages – even after close to a dozen edits. I had zero interest in divorcing myself completely from my emotions and writing a "just the facts" account of what occurred. Fuck that. After all, this is *my* story, not hers. But when I consider what I've written, what I've omitted, and the time that has gone by from then until now, when I am once again happy and in love and teaching and parenting and playing music and writing, I am left with the feeling that I still have one unresolved matter.

It has to do with a small band of persons I've either directly written about in *Land of July*, or whose identities I concealed with pseudonyms. The matter can likely be summed up with any number of words depicting how I feel about their contributions to what became my story. Heartbroken. Bewildered. Disgusted. It's true that within my story I made known my anguish and disbelief over how this band of persons came to regard me. So perhaps this epilogue appears redundant. It's not. Nor is it my intention to create some sort of angry postscript that houses my contempt in one convenient place. Its purpose, then, is simple: I have more to say on the matter.

For every Tom Scarice, or Jude, or Martha, or Aim, the woman who loves anagrams, there have been countless voices, some hushed and anonymous, but most of them bright and comforting and by my side, that have offered me and Robbie and Riley their shoulder, their friendship, their compassion. I've thanked them all. And I'll warmly thank them again. They understood that when a man is down and broken and watching his own life spill out onto the world's stage in messy, permanent blots, the best they can do is psych themselves up, puff up their chests, and do what they can to scare the hell out of his awful loneliness. God bless their instincts.

The people who found themselves involved in my life, whether by choice or by chance, naturally have had their own story to tell. It's easy to imagine them confiding in their family and friends about what went down. I picture my supporters using phrases like "poor bastard" before solemnly shaking their heads and perhaps mumbling a little prayer for me and my kids under their breath. I have an equally easy time suspecting that a few jokes were made at my expense; knowing the jocular tendencies of at least a handful of my male friends, it's more than likely they found the humor in a local sex scandal. Who could blame them?

What's nearly impossible for me to conjure is what someone like Tom Scarice had to say before and after his machination that saw me out of a job. Now, the man is as polished as fine china, so there's zero chance he would ever be without what would surely sound like a lucid explanation – not that he would ever find himself in the position of having to offer one. Still, what would the superintendent of Madison schools say? That I was arrested and proved an embarrassment to the district? That my teaching had suffered? That I breached his investigation that was as rigged and as transparent as they come. I have no argument to make for these claims; they're all true. And I'd make myself sick if I veered into some didactic rant about sympathy and second chances. There should therefore be nothing left to say. What's done is done. Accept it. Well, I have. But not without at least taking the opportunity to more fully come to terms with the characters in my story. Maybe this afterword will come off like an attempt to have the last word. Or like some passive aggressive juvenilia when I point out the irony or ineptitude that my immediate replacement at DHHS read my classes a pornographic short story called "A Real Doll" by A.M. Homes. And that the man who was eventually hired as my replacement – and who still holds the job at the time of this writing – was the subject of a sex–related scandal at his previous school.

Maybe it's all for the best. Maybe Tom did me a favor in the end. I vacillate on these points. Part of me remembers how hard it was to return each day and be the source of such shock and pity by so many. But there's also my dashed dream of teaching in the very school Robbie and Riley will someday attend. I was looking forward to that more than I can possibly express.

I've run into Tom a few times since our final meeting at central office. He's now a Madison resident, so I need to warm up to the idea of seeing him downtown and at fairs and little league games. Though I'm sure he's writhing in his skin when he spots me, it's impossible to tell. With his expert suavity and politician–like posturing, he says hello and smiles and is just as soon on his way. I'm equally polite; yet I'm tortured on the inside. It's a small miracle that I'm able to keep my mouth shut and contain the geyser that might not drown the man, but might at least ruin his afternoon. I'd risk sounding like a boastful prick in telling him about all the students who visited my home to tell me they missed me. And the letters and phone calls I received from parents who told me they were saddened and appalled over my treatment. I'd tell him about the mother who cried and hugged me in Stop & Shop when she learned I would not be teaching her daughter. And about the woman who came to my yard sale over the summer and shared what she described as a "unanimous opinion" of Madison's central office team. It would be impossible for me to conceal how so many of my former colleagues in the English department have expressed to me their views on what they feel Mr. Scarice has done to the morale and leadership of what was once a fine department.

As for Martha, and Aim, the woman who loves anagrams, I could have saved some keyboard strokes by turning them into a composite character. Both women proved to be rather skilled opportunists. They manufactured an opening and slithered their way into my life without provocation. Both figured that glomming onto a wildly unpopular cause might result in unlikely heroine status rather than social suicide, which I've learned has been the case. Both have taken on Machiavellian proportions in my mind. These women are educators and mothers who elected to be a part of something no healthy or sane person would willingly touch. I honestly see them as predatory as I do the central antagonist in *Land of July*.

I've been asked countless times my view on the support and even cheers my ex-wife managed to chalk up through Facebook and other social media outlets. My response was always twofold: 1) As for the *technology*, I don't engage in any of those dead-end pastimes and 2) As for the *people*, they're misguided anomalies who have confounded the absolute hell out of those who see this catastrophe for what it is: entirely devoid of a gray area. I can only suppose that these individuals were so bored that they became swept up in some salacious wave of voyeurism. They were safely moored to their own life, which must have looked far more appealing than Allison's, when they let their commentary ring out for all the world to see. "I applaud your strength and perseverance – both are a testament to your character." "You're a good person and a good mother." "Don't let yourself be defined by this – keep looking ahead towards the future."

It's easy to predict that such comments were written by those who forced themselves to vilify me. Believing that the husband was abusive or neglectful provides at least a modicum of reason to an otherwise inexplicable turn of events. What layperson among us can claim they truly understand mental illness or serious self-sabotage? There's this to ponder as well as the hypothetical moral quandary that puts *me* in the role of the offender. It's hardly worth expounding on the obvious that I would be persona non grata faster than it would take for me to change my name and zip code. What I'll do instead is share, verbatim, one of my ex-wife's Facebook posts from June 28th, our wedding anniversary:

Ten years ago today I married my best friend. I can't believe a decade has passed. I feel so grateful for all the good times and the beautiful life we've created together. I couldn't ask for a better friend, husband, or father for my children.

Then there's Jude, cancer survivor and unabashed turncoat. He received little mention in *Land of July*. Yet he looms as one of the biggest disappointments in my twisted saga. I suppose I should be grateful that he's my only friend casualty. That's not a bad ratio. But it still stings like hell.

A story I excluded from *Land of July* is one that recalls the last conversation Jude and I ever shared with one another. It was the end of a work week when I visited his wife's classroom; the purpose of my visit was to ask her why she thought her husband wouldn't provide me with the character reference I needed for my divorce attorney. She threw her arms up in the air and stated what I already knew, which was that Jude was obstinate. Later that day, on the third floor of DHHS, during passing, Jude accosted me and told me to never speak to his wife again about the letter business or anything else for that matter. He said I had crossed a line and acted inappropriately and had embarrassed myself. Then he stormed off down the hall. With the feeling that I had just been admonished by a parent for stealing or smoking, I bowed my head a little and made my way back to my room. I can still recall student onlookers and their quizzical expressions over what they had just witnessed.

Jude's inability to comprehend my pathos was stunning to me. There I was, in tatters, trying to maintain dignity after having my universe blowtorched, and he could only regard me as some fucking nuisance. His feelings towards me were cemented when I eventually learned what he told a mutual friend. They were talking about the scandal one afternoon when Jude apparently shook his head, scoffed a little and said, "I want Rob to just...to just go away." I can only imagine how he felt when his wish came true a short while later.

I've heard many say how there was never a manual on how to deal with such a calamity. I'll admit that I may have even said this myself on occasion to possibly justify my own behavior. It's a statement that can elicit only a sober reaction – a lot of affirmative head nods are what I mostly recall. And though it's certainly a truism, it's equally a cop out. Cop outs are fine, I suppose, when they're defaults – when intentions are pure, yet actions remain inert.

Some of my closest friends were lost when it came to how to console me. My family, too. This makes perfect sense. They lacked the muscle memory to tell them what to say and do and how to think and feel. I can grasp all of that. Hell, I was in the same predicament. But when conscious choices were made to act with malice or insensitivity, when there were designs to conspire against me, to weaken me, to set up further insurmountable obstacles, to work towards relegating me to second-class citizen status, well, I guess all I can say today, years later, after my rage and sorrow have been blunted, when I can breathe again and take in the full panorama of that time, is thank you for those invaluable hard luck lessons on humanity. I plan to use them all to become a better parent, a better man, a better writer. Up until those points in my life, I was sheltered, privileged even, in my blissful naiveté, having only second hand knowledge of such contemptuous behavior.

We perpetuate our stories throughout the years by continuing to believe in them. Not only that, but we sharpen them with each retelling. And they become finer and more potent and thus more believable. This makes them easier to sell. And we quietly rejoice over this. After all, each of us are story-salesmen at our cores. We hustle every day, selling our little tales to each other with a wink and a nod and a hope in our hearts that we'll be believed and perhaps even asked to tell another and another and another.

As for me, I've done my part. I've told my story. Whether I've *sold* it may be another matter altogether. I understand this. But I refuse to think about that. I'm finished. I've moved on.

About the Author

Robert M. Marchese is a writer, musician, and English teacher who lives in CT with his family. Marchese's previous works include a novel entitled *Nine Lies*, also published by Black Rose Writing. *Land of July*, Marchese's second book, is the recipient of the not at all coveted Pen/Corvino Award for Nonfiction, as well as the runner up for the ignoble D. Earles Medal for First-Time Memoirists. He enjoys music, traveling, and literature. Robert hopes to never write another memoir again.